WRITTEN BY : Jin Liang
TRANSLATED BY : Zhou Jian, Zhao Yahui

Bronze Ware

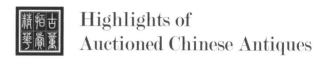

Highlights of
Auctioned Chinese Antiques

Hunan Fine Arts Publishing House

图书在版编目（CIP）数据

中国古董拍卖精华. 铜器 : 英文 / 金良编著. -- 长沙 : 湖南美术出版社,
2012.3
ISBN 978-7-5356-5185-3

Ⅰ.①中… Ⅱ.①金… Ⅲ.①铜器（考古）－拍卖－中国－图集 Ⅳ.
①F724.59-64

中国版本图书馆CIP数据核字(2012)第032449号

Bronze Ware of Highlights of Auctioned Chinese Antiques

Publisher: Li Xiaoshan

Supervisor: Zhang Xiao, Yan Hua

Author: Jin Liang

Translator: Zhou Jian, Zhao Yahui

Editor in charge: Liu Haizhen, Liu Yingzheng

Proof-reading: Chen Yinxia

Graphic Design: Xiao Ruizi, Hu Shanshan,
Shu Xiaowen

Plate-making: Sun Yan, Xiong Jie

English Evaluation: Xiao Fang

Publishing and Distribution House: Hunan Fine Arts
Publishing House (No.622, Section 1, Eastern Beltway
2, Changsha, Hunan, China)

Distributor: Hunan Xinhua Bookstore Co., Ltd.

Printing House: Shenzhen Hua Xin Printing Co., Ltd.

Size: 787 × 1092 1/16

Sheets: 10

Version: May 2012, first edition;
        May 2012, first printing

ISBN: ISBN 978-7-5356-5185-3

Price: USD $19.90/ CNY ￥98.00

CONTENTS

Ⅱ. Musical Instruments

Ⅲ. Weapons

Ⅳ. Bronze Mirrors

Ⅴ. Religious statues and appliances

VII. Others

Guide to the Use of This Series

1. "Highlights of Auctioned Chinese Antiques" comprises five volumes, namely, "Bamboo, Wood, Ivory and Horn Carvings", "Porcelain", "Jadeware", "Bronzeware" and "Ancient Furniture". Each volume contains around 150 representative items put up for auction from 1995 to 2010 at auctions held by dozens of auction companies from cities like New York, Nagel, London, Hong Kong, Macau, Taipei, Beijing, Shanghai, Tianjin, Nanjing, Guangzhou, Kunming, Chengdu and Jinan. The selection of the items is based on the style, texture, form, decorative pattern, workmanship, function, cultural implication and value of the antiques in question, including some items which have not yet been transacted.

2. Each volume retains the original record of auctions and the items are arranged in order of dynasty, name, dimension, transaction price (or estimate price), auction company, date of transaction and item analysis.

3. Due to different origins of auction companies, the prices of the antiques in US dollar, Euro, Great Britain Pound, Hong Kong dollar or Taiwan dollar, have been converted into RMB according to current exchange rates.

Preface

On Chinese BronezWare Market

Jin Liang

To have a clear understanding of the development of Chinese bronze ware market, one has to have enough understanding of the features and value of Chinese bronze wares, and the formation of its market at first.

Ⅰ. The History and Present Situation of Chinese Bronze Ware Collection

The earliest record about excavation of Chinese bronze wares was found in the Han Dynasty, which was regarded as an auspicious sign at that time. It is recorded in Historic Record-Regulations of Offering Sacrifices to Heaven and Earth that once Emperor Wu got an ancient bronze ware, and asked Mr. Shaojun for its origin. Mr. Shaojun answered that this item was once put on the Bai Qin by Duke Huan of Qi. Confirmed by the later found inscription on it, the item did belong to Duke Huan of Qi. Everyone was shocked and thought Mr. Shaojun was immortal so that he would live for such a long life and know things happened hundreds of years ago. Another record is found in Book of Former Han-Treatise on Sacrifice, which is about where to put a bronze ware discovered and presented to Emperor Xuan. Some ministers declared that this bronze ware should be consecrated in the royal ancestral temple. But the governor of the capital city, Mr. Zhang Chang declared that it was not proper to be placed there, since, according to the inscription, it was an article in commemoration of one subject's ancestor honored by Emperor zhou. Another record is found in Book of Later Han Dynasty-Biography of General Dou Xian, which says that General Dou Xian found a bronze ware in the battle with Hun army, and presented it to Emperor He. In Book of Liang-Biography of Liu Xian, it is recorded that someone from Kingdom of Wei presented a bronze ware to Emperor Liang. There were some words of the inscription that could not be recognized by most of the people. Liu Xian, however, could read the whole inscription easily and accurately tell the producing year and month of the item. In Book of Liang-Biography of Liu Yao, there was a discussion between Liu Yao and Shen Yue about bronze wine vessels used in sacrificial ceremonies. Liu Yao said that, "In ancient time, the wine vessel used in a ceremony was made of wood and in the shape of a bird or an animal. The top of the bird or the back of the animal was holed in order to hold wine. It was said that one senior official in Kingdom of Qi named Zi Wei sent a bronze wine vessel to his daughter as a wedding gift. The vessel was in the shape of an ox. In the Jin Dynasty, a thief named Cao Yi robbed the tomb of King Jinggong of Kingdom of Qi, and got two ox-shaped bronze vessels. "A scholar in the Song Dynasty named Wang Yinglin wrote in his book Yu Hai -Collection of Jade that," In October of the 13th year of Kaiyuan Reign, 5 precious bronze tripods were discovered and presented to the Emperor. 4 of them had inscriptions." Generally speaking, bronze wares unearthed during this period of time were presented to emperors and preserved in the royal palace. Ruan Yuan, a scholar in the Qing Dynasty, concluded that, " Since bronze wares were rare from the Tang Dynasty to the Han Dynasty, ancient bronze wares were gained by chance, and would be recorded and referred as a token of good fortune. Those who could recognize the inscriptions on the bronze wares were generally referred as gifted people."

The market of Chinese bronze ware was formed in the Song Dynasty, which was the first zenith in the development of Chinese bronze ware collection. According to History of the Song Dynasty-Treaties on Rites, the Bureau of Rites was established at the beginning of the Song Dynasty, specifying in the collection of ancient bronze wares and in the production of the bronze ware imitating in ancient styles. A bureau for the production of ritual objects was later established in the royal palace, hence the large production of bronze wares in ancient styles. Ouyang Xiu, in the postscript of his Collection of Ancient Antiques, mentioned that in the reign of Emperor Taizu, a craftsman named Wang Pu was very good at making chimes, in the same style of those in the Zhou Dynasty. In the 3rd year of Xianping Reign, one ancient bronze object was presented to the emperor from Gangzhou area. This object, cube-shaped and four-footed, had an inscription of 21 characters, which was identified as a bronze Yan (one kind of ancient cooking vessel with a grid on it) made by Mr. Shi Xinfu. Emperor Huizong was fond of ancient antiques, and ordered the royal workshop to produce bronze wares according to the ancient style. It was recorded that the royal workshop produced the fine and exquisite Dasheng Chime, based on the style of Gongshu Bell in the Spring and Autumn Period. During the whole Song Dynasty, on the one hand, the imperial family had played a very important and efficient role in the collection of bronze wares. It had been recorded that there were merely 500 bronze wares at the beginning of Daguan Reign. The number of the collected bronze wares had reached 6,000 in the Zhenghe Reign. On the other hand, the high officials, aristocrats and famous scholars of this time were also fond of the collection of bronze wares. According to Picture Album of Antiques of the Northern Song Dynasty and the Continuation of Picture Album of Antiques of the Southern Song Dynasty, there were over 40 famous collectors of bronze ware in the Northern Song Dynasty, while over 30 in the Southern Song Dynasty. A lot of famous scholars, such as Kou Zhun, Wen Yanbo, Liu Chang, Su Shi, Li Gonglin, Ouyang Xiu, Lü Dalin, Zhao Mingcheng, boasted of the collection of bronze wares. Su Shi had the famous Bell of King Chu in his collections. Liu Chang, a famous scholar in Jixian College and the owner of a large number of bronze wares, wrote a book titled Collection of Bronze Wares in the Early Qin Dynasty. Liu Chang was crazy about 11 bronze wares that had inscriptions out of all his collections. He had spent plenty of time in appreciating and studying them, till the end of his life. He told his offsprings that "Do not forget to use these 11 bronze wares to offer sacrifices to me after my death". Ruan Yuan concluded that "Starting from the Northern Song Dynasty, as more bronze wares were excavated from ancient tombs, bronze wares were no longer regarded as auspicious items. Scholars came to appreciate these bronze wares and research them with more accuracy".

As Wang Guowei (a famous scholar in the late Qing Dynasty) said, the terminologies of ancient ritual bronze objects were determined in the Song Dynasty. "Each bronze item had its name in ancient time, but without a specific explanation. Scholars in the Song Dynasty borrowed these names to describe the found bronze wares according to the size of each item. That is why the name of the bronze ware, such as Jue, Gu, Zhi, Jiao and Jia, was established and used till today. " It is in the Song Dynasty that the foundation of the bronze ware research was established. The method of describing and recording of bronze wares was first demonstrated by Picture Album of Antiques and Picture Catalogue of Antique Collection in Xuanhe Reign, which is still a valuable reference for the research of bronze wares today.

The Appreciation and collection of bronze wares experienced another zenith in the Qing Dynasty, due to Emperor Qianglong's great advocacy. Besides the imperial family, high officials and scholars were also fond of the collection of bronze wares, and produced a large number of collectors during that time. In 1749, Emperor Qianlong ordered one of his officials Liang Shizheng to compile Xi Qing Gu Jian, a 2-part 40-volume catalogue of the appreciation of imperial collections of antiques, following the style of Picture Catalogue of Antique Collection in Xuanhe Reign. This book includes descriptions of 1436 bronze wares collected by the imperial family. Xi Qing Xu Jian, another 2-part 40-volume catalogue of the appreciation of antiques of imperial collections was compiled by Wang Jie, containing descriptions of 1642 items. The collection of antiques in Ningshou Palace was also compiled into a 16-volume catalogue, called Appreciation of Antiques in Ningshou Palace, which contains 600 bronze wares and 101 bronze mirrors. These three books roughly reflect the whole collection of bronze wares of the imperial family in the Qing Dynasty.

The collection of high ranking officials and literary scholars of the Qing Dynasty is more significant in the archaeological research. Qian Dian (1741—1806), a native Jiading people, wrote a 4-volume Research and Description of the Antiques of the Collection from Shi Liu Chang Yue Tang, containing 25 bronze articles from the Shang and Zhou Dynasties, and 24 other antiques. Ruan Yuan (1764—1849), a successful candidate in the highest imperial examinations in Qianlong Reign, had been appointed subsequently as the vice-minister of the Ministry of Revenue, War, and Works, Governor of Yunnan and Guizhou Province, and Senior Imperial Advisor. Ruan Yuan was also a great antiquarian at the time, and, based on his own collections, he compiled two books: Catalogue of Collection of Ji Gu Zhai, including 74 pieces of bells and tripods; and Inscription on the Bronze Ware from Ji Gu Zhai, including 446 pieces of bronze wares from Shang and Zhou Dynasties and 105 pieces of other antiques. As a private collector, Ruan Yuan was unmatchable for his personal collection of bronze wares. Among Ruan Yuan's collections, there used to be two Leis of the Marquis of Qi, which were regarded as treasures ever since then. Wu Yun, another famous collector of antiques, owned these two Leis later, and renamed his home as "House of Two Leis". Chen Jieqi (1813—1884), a native people of Shandong Province, was appointed as a member of Imperial Academy. Chen was crazy about antiques all his life, and had written a lot of books about the appreciation of bronze wares and the research and explanation of the inscriptions on them. Chen was also famous to be the owner of Mao Gong Tripod and many other precious bronze antiques from Shang and Zhou Dynasties. Many other scholars of this time had written books on the collection and research of bronze wares. Among all these books, Fang Shuiruiyi's 30-volume Study and Explanation of the Inscription of the Bronze Wares from Zhui Yi Zhai is comprehensive and valuable, for it includes over 1,000 pieces of bronze items, and adds explanations to all the famous inscriptions. Especially, on the preface of the book, Fang had recorded faithfully and carefully the collection and trading of all the famous bronze wares before the Qing Dynasty.

Pan Zuyin, a minister of the Ministry of Works in the Qing Dynasty, was fond of the collection of bronze wares. Among his collections, the most famous ones were Da Ke Tripod and Da Yu Tripod of the Western

Zhou Dynasty. Da Ke Tripod, with the height of 93.1 cm and the weight of 201.5kg, was fully decorated with transformed beast face patterns. With three feet and two upright ears, this tripod fully exhibits the beauty and the elegance of Chinese bronze wares. An inscription of 290 characters was neatly engraved on the inner surface of the tripod. Da Yu Tripod, 101.9 cm in height and 133.5 kg in weight, has three feet and a pair of big upright ears. This tripod, magnificent in form and simplified in design, has a precious inscription of 291 characters. Both of these two bronze articles had been coveted by many bureaucrats and merchants both at home and abroad. After Pan's death, these two tripods had been transferred to his hometown in Suzhou. Pan's offspring refused the many offers to buy these two tripods from U.S, Japan, and high-ranking officials of the Kuomintang Government. In the Anti-Japanese War, Suzhou was captured by the Japanese army. Pan's family buried these two tripods deeply in the yard in order to avoid Japanese's ransacking, which sometimes took place seven times a day. In 1952, Pan's offsprings donated Da Ke Tripod to Shanghai Museum, and Da Yu Tripod to the National Museum of Chineses History.

At the beginning of 20th Century, Chinese antique market became very active, stimulated by the discoveries of bamboo slips of Juyan, Buddha scriptures of Dunhuang Grotto and the Ruin of Yin, the capital city of the Shang Dynasty. A large number of great collectors emerged during this period of time. Most of these collectors were either high-ranking officials or rich merchants, such as Duan Fang, the Governor of Liangjiang Province; Li Jingfang, the Chinese Minister to Japan; Liu Huizhi, General Manager of the National Industrial Bank of China; Luo Zhenyu and Rong Geng, archaeologists ; Huang Bochuan and Sun Qiufan, owners of the curiosity shop in Liulichang (a famous district in Beijing that is known for a series of stores selling various craftwork, artworks, and antiques), etc. These collectors had collection of dozens of, or even hundreds of, ancient or newly unearthed antiques. They shared information, rubbings and research results of antiques, and helped each other to compile books and catalogues of antiques. Thus a circle of collectors had naturally formed among them.

In 1860, the Eight-Power Allied Forces captured Beijing and looted Yuanmingyuan Imperial Garden. Since then, Chinese bronze antiques had became known to the world and had been bought in large number worldwide, and an international market for Chinese bronze ware was formed in the early 20th Century. A lot of private collections found their ways to foreign museums or art galleries. In 1890, over 120 pieces of bronze antiques were unearthed in the Famen Temple of Fufeng County in Shaanxi Province, including Da Ke tripods, Xiao Ke Tripods, Ke Xus and Ke Bells. For Ke bells, two are preserved in Shanghai Museum, one in Tianjin Art Museum, one in Neiraku Museum of Japan, and one in Fujii Saiseikai Yurinkan Museum of Art of Japan. There were inscriptions of 79characters engraved on these five bells. However, as the bells are preserved in different places, it is not convenient for the research work. Same situation takes place in some other bronze wares, for example, the cover and the body of the bronze wares, or the same series of bronze wares are preserved in different locations. Mr Chen Mengjia, a famous historian, once conducted tour to Europe and America for the investigation of Chinese bronze wares preserved in these foreign countries. He found that there were over 800 pieces of bronze wares preserved in the museums of the United States. In the preface to Catalogue of the Bronze Wares Looted by American Imperialists, it says, "This catalogue contains 845 pieces of bronze ritual objects dated back to Shang and Zhou Dynasties. This catalogue is finished by Mr. Chen Mengjia of our museum. Mr. Chen spent more than 10 years in the US in visiting different museums, universities and various antique shops. To compile this catalogue, Mr. Chen took photos of and measured the bronze wares, made rubbings for the inscriptions and investigated the origins of the objects. Except for a few, most of the objects had been closely observed by Mr. Chen."

Since 1949, many history and art museums had been established in various areas of China. A lot of bronze wares flocked to these museums, as the donation of the private collectors was encouraged by Chinese government at that time. Li Yinxuan, a grandson of Li Hongzhang's fifth younger brother, one of the few but maybe the most famous private collectors, donated all his collections to Shanghai Museum during the period of the Great Culture Revolution.

Since 1980, the collection of antiques has become popular in China. However, the market of bronze wares hasn't restored its momentum in bloom yet. In the early period of 20th century, a bronze ware of the Zhou Dynasty could be traded for a pile of porcelain produced in imperial kilns in Qianlong Reign in Liulichang. However, even the price of a nice glass snuff bottle would be higher than that of a bronze ware of the Zhou Dynasty at present. It is mentioned by some people sentimentally that, "Bronze wares from Xia, Shang and Zhou Dynasties are precious rarities. It is so sad that the price of a bronze ware from these three dynasties is lower than that of the porcelain of the Qing Dynasty. "In spite of that, bronze wares were bided in stunning prices in overseas market. For example, New York Christie's organized an auction sale especially for Chinese porcelain and ancient handcrafts in the spring of 2001. Out of 5 bronze wares at this sale, a bronze Mintianquan Lei (body) from the Shang Dynasty was transacted at the price of 9,240,000 US dollars in New York. This is the new record of the price of the oriental handcraft. On March 31st, 2007, at the spring auction sale organized by New York Sotheby's, a square Jia with owl patterns was transacted at the price of 8,104,000 US dollars. In March of 2007, at the European Antique Fair hold in Maastricht of Netherlands, a bronze tripod inlaid with gold and turquoise and in the shape of tapir was transacted at the price of 12,000,000 US dollars. This is the highest price in the history of auctions for Chinese bronze wares, proving the unequaled artistic value of Chinese bronze wares. Chongyuan Auction (Shanghai) hold an auction on January 5th, 2006 in Shanghai, and a bronze ewer from the mid-Zhou Dynasty, which was called Zhou Yi Ewer as these two Chinese characters were found in the inscriptions engraved, was sold at the hammer price of 26, 400,000 RMB. This is the highest price of bronze wares in Chinese mainland. All these examples show that the market of Chinese bronze wares is taking a gradual turn toward bloom.

II. The Uniqueness of Chinese Bronze Wares

The uniqueness of Chinese bronze wares helps the formation of the international market.

As various regions of the world entered into Bronze Age in different times, the technology of smelting and casting experienced an unbalanced development in various regions. People in South Iran, Turkey and Mesopotamia have a history of over 5,000 years of using bronze wares. People from Europe had learned wax-lost approach for casting bronze wares around 10th century BC. People from the Indus River Valley mastered advanced bronze casting technologies around 4,000 years ago. They applied hot-processing, cold-processing and welding to cast bronze wares. From around 1567 BC to 1085 BC, the Egyptian had mastered foot-blower, one advanced equipment for smelting in that time. People from America mastered technology of smelting and casting comparatively later, around Christian era. Being one of the first to use bronze wares, Chinese people's technology of bronze ware manufacture had been at the forefront of the world for a long time.

Before entering into Bronze Age, Chinese people had a long time of accumulation of technology and experience for bronze ware casting. Based on the archaeological discoveries in the Banpo Cultural Relic of Xi'an and Yangshao Cultural Relic of Lintong, Chinese people of around 6,000 years ago had impure brass chips. This discovery was controversial till the discovery in the Sanlihe Cultural Relic of Shandong Province. Two bronze awls were unearthed in Sanlihe, which, after the scientific analysis, were copper-zinc alloys. Further research found out that there were cooper-zinc and cooper-zinc-lead polymetallic ores in this region. During this period of time, brass was easily obtained through a simple method. It is around 2000 BC that Chinese people entered into Bronze Age. And Chinese people used brass, red bronze and bronze to produce bronze objects, through methods of hot-processing and cold-processing. The bronze awls found in Sanlihe were products of this period. The solidified liquid copper found in Longshan Cultural Relic of Henan Province, after analysis, is the red bronze with the purity of 95%. Qijia Culture Relic of Gansu and Qinghai Province already had bronze products. Various knives, axes, chisels and daggers that made of bronze or red bronze were unearthed from the Qijia Cultural Relic.

Based on the materials at hand, we can summarize the following characteristics of the bronze wares of this period: co-existence of bronze and red bronze, excavated from several tombs from Qijia Culture Relic in Gansu Province, Qinghai and Ningxia Province, were knives, chisels, drills, rings and mirrors, some of which were made of bronze, some of red bronze; some advanced technologies of this time, such as hammering and model casting, were applied; most of these bronze wares were articles or tools of everyday use; bronze ware of this time didn't reflect the social status and common people could afford bronze wares, as bronze wares were discovered in some small tombs; bronze wares of this time were simply decorated or without decoration at all. Some bronze mirrors from this period of time were decorated merely with star-and-stripe patterns and triangle patterns.

Relics of bronze casting workshop and workshop-style firm were found in the Erlitou Cultural Relic of Henan Province. Furnaces, clinkers, smelters and dozens of pottery models were excavated there. Exquisite decorative patterns were found on these pottery models. It was in this period of time that the technology was developed from casting simple tools and weapons to casting complicate containers. Bronze wares discovered from this period of time were complicate vessels (Jue, Jia, He, tripod), musical instruments (small bells), weapons (Ge, Qi) and various tools (small knife, Ben, chisel, awl and saw). Decorative plaques and bronze bubbles were inlaid with turquoise. Generally speaking, bronze wares from Erlitou Culture Relic have no decorative patterns. However, one or two rows of nipple patterns have been found on the bodies of some tripods of this period. Some gibbosities in the shape of a small cake are found on the bellies of tripods, which can be regarded as the origin of the decorative patterns of the early Shang Dynasty. Although animal pattern has not been discovered on the ritual bronze objects from Erlitou Culture Relic yet, we can not say that there are no such decorations on the bronze wares of this time, as distorted animal pattern has been found inside the bronze Ge from this period of time. Erlitou Culture Relic existed roughly in the period of the Xia Dynasty, thus, the bronze wares found from this relic is regarded as the bronze wares of the Xia Dynasty. With the appearance of bronze ritual objects, China entered into Bronze Age with Chinese characteristics.

Compared with the bronze culture of other parts of the world, Chinese bronze ware is unique for its special function. To be specific, Chinese bronze ware represents sovereignty and is the symbol of social status.

In ancient Chinese history, it is record that "in the Xia Dynasty, nine tripods were cast", which fully embodied the social value of bronze wares in Chinese history. In the 21st Century BC, the ruler of the Xia Dynasty cast nine huge tripods out of the bronze distributed by various dukes, with the names of mountains and rivers of the nine parts of the empire engraved on the surfaces. Since then, "Nine Tripods" had become the symbol of the sovereignty of the whole country. One who owned these nine tripods could wield the highest political power of the country. A saying goes like this "Owning 'Nine Tripods', one has the country; losing 'Nine Tripods', one loses the ruling of the country." After the perilsh of the Xia Dynasty, the ruler of the Shang Dynasty owned these nine tripods. At the end of the Shang Dynasty, Emperor Zhouwu, united all the other dukes, overthrew the ruling of Emperor Zhou of the Shang Dynasty, and established the Zhou Dynasty. The "Nine Tripods", thereafter, became the treasure of the Zhou Dynasty. In the Spring and Autumn Period, the power of the emperor of the Zhou Dynasty declined, as the power of the dukes increased. Kingdom of Qi, Song, Jin, Qin and Chu successfully declared hegemony over other kingdoms, and wanted to seize the power from the emperor of the Zhou Dynasty. In 606 BC, in the course of a battle with northern minorities, Duke Zhuang of the Kingdom of Chu led his army in marching through the suburbs of the Capital City. Duke Zhuang had a military exercise to show off his power. Emperor Ding of the Zhou Dynasty sent Wang Sunman to send greetings and gifts to the army. Duke Zhuang took this opportunity and asked for the weight and size of these nine tripods Wang Sunman, knowing the real intention of Duke Zhuang, said sharply, "The rise and fall of a country is decided by the moral power and Heaven's will, rather than the owning of these nine tripods. The Zhou Dynasty is declining, but is still protected by the Heaven. It is totally improper for you to know the size and weight of these nine tripods."

After the fall of the Zhou Dynasty, the nine tripods were obtained by the Duke of Kingdom of Qin. In 296 BC,

Duke Zhao sent all these nine tripods back to Kingdom of Qin. When they were crossing the Si River, one tripod was lost into the river and could not be found. Emperor Shihuang of the Qin Dynasty, after conquering all the other six kingdoms and unifying the whole China, sent over 1,000 men to find this tripod in the Si River, but could not get it. However, the stories of "Inquiring for the weight of the nine tripod in Central Plains" and "Finding the lost tripod in the River of Si" have been handed down through history records or oral literature. A brick with a portrait, unearthed from Wuzhaishan of Shandong Province, has vividly recorded the image of the unsuccessful endeavor of Emperor Shihuang of the Qin Dynasty. In the portrait, as the tripod comes out of the river, a dragon suddenly appears and bites the rope around the tripod, which causes the tripod to sink into the river again.

Governing the country though rites is the unique characteristic of ancient Chinese rulers to wield the political power. A system of rites, represented by Rites of the Zhou Dynasty, had embodied throughout the political, economic, military and cultural aspects of ancient Chinese society for thousands of years. Based on the confusion ideology of the early Qin Dynasty, rite-music culture is founded on the difference between human beings and animals. Confucius, Mencious and Xun Zi believed that rites and music set human beings from other animals. It was rites that transformed a primitive society into a society that could tell the differences between the emperors and the subjects, the high and the low, the superiority and the inferiority, and the senior and the younger, that transformed a person whose action was controlled by the physical desire to a person whose action was decided by social norms, and that led to a ordered and harmonious community and a civilized world. Bronze ware was an important tool to conduct governance to a country through rites during that time. According to Spring and Autumn Annals — The Commentary of Gongyang, it was proper for the emperor to use 9 tripods, duke 7 tripods, minister 5 tripods, intelligentsia 3 tripods or 1 tripod at that time. According to the archaeological discovery, tripod and Gui were used together, representing the tradition of emphasizing food in the Zhou Dynasty. However, tripods of odd number were always found together with Guis of even number, such as 9 tripods and 8 Guis, or 7 tripods and 6 Guis were found together. "Setting tripod and sacrificial utensil is an expression of rites, so as to tell the difference between grades and hierarchies." Aristocrats were able to use these bronze wares in the ceremony of sacrifice, feast, combat and funeral. While common people would not use bronze wares, as "Rites do not extend to the common people" .

The system of rites in the Zhou Dynasty didn't originate from nowhere. Confucius once said , "It could be proved that the rites of the Shang Dynasty followed those of the Xia Dynasty, with some addition or deduction of the contents; while the rites of the Zhou Dynasty followed those of the Shang Dynasty. The rites that were the same with those of the Zhou Dynasty could be found out through hundreds of years." Archaeological discoveries proved there existed differences between rites of the Shang Dynasty and the Zhou Dynasty. People of the Shang Dynasty applied porcelain or bronze wine vessels as the major rites objects. Gu and Jue, as a set of rites object, were found in some tombs from this period of time. One, two or four sets were found. In the Fuhao tomb of the Shang Dynasty, 53 Gus, 40 Jue, and 12 Jias were unearthed, some of which were in the shape of a square.

Difference in number reflected the difference in social status. "People of the Shang Dynasty respected gods, and rulers would lead common people to hold sacrificial ceremonies for gods." Most of the wine vessels excavated from this period of time were devoted to the gods. In the late Shang Dynasty, musical instruments had already been used as rites objects. A five-piece bronze cymbal was unearthed from the Fuhao tomb of the Shang Dynasty.

Based on the history of the fall of the Shang Dynasty, rulers of the Zhou Dynasty, on the other hand, thought that wine was an important reason that led to the perish of the shang Dynasty, and announced prohibition against wine. In the mid-Zhou Dynasty, wine vessels had greatly disappeared and tripods had become the major rites objects. During this time, difference in number and kinds of musical instruments also reflected the social statuses of the people, and different music was supposed to be played in various situations. In the same situation, musical instruments and rites objects played different roles. Having meals with tripods holding food and resonant bells being played were the typical reflections of the function of these bronze wares.

Besides tripod and Gui, other bronze wares used together with them were also regarded as rites objects in ancient China. Some bronze weapons and tools also fell into the category of rites objects. Chinese bronze wares are not only material goods, but also spiritual ones, embedded with the worship, expectation and ideology of various nobilities. The beauty of Chinese bronze wares is the connotation of rites attached to it.

III. The Artistic Feature of Chinese Bronze Wares

Due to its artistic glamour, Chinese bronze wares has formed an international trading market. The artistic glamour is vividly exhibited in the following three aspects: ingenious design, complicated decoration and various inscriptions.

Different kinds of Chinese bronze wares were unearthed in large number and with various designs. There are bronze wine vessels, food containers, water vessels, musical instruments, weapons, tools, carriages and chariots, daily utensils, coins and seals. For the category of wine vessel, there are over 20 kinds, such as Jiao, Dan, Jia, Zun, Hu, You, Square Yi, Gong, Lei, He and spoon, etc. Each kind of bronze ware exhibits unique features in different times, and the same kind of bronze ware of the same age, if they were from different locations, might be designed variously. Chinese bronze ware, being of great variety and ingenuous design, is full of the value of artistic appreciation. Taking tripod as an example, there are round, square and animal-shaped tripods. Square Tripod with Four Rams is the largest one in size among all the discovered square bronze tripods of the Shang Dynasty at present. This tripod has a huge mouth with a flared lip, a long neck and a high ring foot. The neck of the tripod is decorated with banana-leaf patterns, triangular dragon patterns and beast face patterns. On the four corners of the shoulders, there are four protruding rams'heads with curly horns. The rams'chests form the belly of the tripod, with the legs of the rams extending down to the ring foot. The chests and the necks of the rams are decorated with fish-scale patterns, the flanks are decorated with beautiful phoenix-with-high-crest patterns, and the ring foot is also decorated with dragon patterns. On the shoulders there are high-relief designs of dragons, with the two-horned dragon head projecting out. The shoulders, belly and ring foot together form four big curly-horn rams. There are edges on the corners and in the middle of each side of the belly, which make the design of the whole object vivid. After analysis, this square tripod is manufactured through separated casting. That is to say heads and horns of the rams were first cast, and then they were set on the exterior structure and the whole casting went through. The advanced casting technology of ancient Chinese has been fully exhibited on this tripod. This article has combined the technologies of line carving, relief caving and circular carving, planar decorative patterns with solid sculpture, and the usages of the vessel and animal shapes. The tripod is a perfect fusion of moulding and artistic design, representing the very best of bronze-making by the traditional clay mould technique, and is regarded as "the masterpiece of ancient Chinese bronze ware ".

There is a large number of striking ancient Chinese bronze wares, with unique design. Tiger-shaped You is the treasure from the late Shang Dynasty. There are only two pieces of Tiger-shaped You unearthed till now, one of which is preserved in Sen-oku Hakuko Museum of Japan, and the other of which in Paris Municipal Museum for Oriental Art Gallery (Cernuschi Museum). The surfaces of the items are black, with some greenish marks of rusty copper. These Yous have complicated decorations, with people and beast as their themes, expressing a mysterious idea.

The bronze holy trees, unearthed from Sanxingdui Culture Relic, are various in design, but roughly same in structure. The under part of the bronze holy tree is cast in the shape of a cloud hill, while the upper part is the trunk that is attached with 9 branches, hanging down in 3 layers. There are birds, dragons, peaches halos and bis on the tree. The structure of the bronze tree is similar to the description in Classics of Mountains and Seas-- East Regions beyond the Seas, "In the Region of Tanggu, there is a place called Fusang, where all the ten suns rest. In the north part of Heichi and in the middle of the river, there is a great tree, with nine suns standing below, while the rest one on the top of the tree, " Birds standing on the tree, together with the halo, has represented the worship to the sun in ancient China. In the fancy world of ancient Sichuan people the bronze tree is which the sun rest on and rise from. The bronze mask excavated from Sanxingdui Cultural Relic, which had been placed on the top of totem-pole, represents one of the major gods whom ancient Sichuan people showed sacrifice to. This bronze mask, with long ears, a big mouth, a high-bridged nose and a huge face, is exaggeratedly manufactured. Especially, the big eyes and the cylinder-shaped and bulged-out pupils are the prominent symbols of the god, and exhibit a striking and irresistible power. This mask is in a sharp contrast to the life-like, well-balanced and solemn-looking bronze mask, just representing the sharp contrast between the human being and the god. According to the Records of Huayang Kingdom-- Records of Kingdom of Shu, there once was a duke named Cancong in ancient Sichuan area, with his eyes bulged out. He declared himself the king of the area. Cancong ordered a stone coffin to be made for himself, and his subjects followed that order after his death. Thereafter, a stone coffin was made for the person with eyes bulged out. Ancient people in Sichuan area regarded the phenomenon of eyes being bulged out as a magical, and used this exaggerated design to express the image of the god in the manufacture of bronze wares.

The bronze ware from ancient Yunnan area was designed as a major item attached with a small statue of animal, or was the combination of the item and the statue of human shape or animal shape. This is a typical feature of the bronze ware of this area, differentiating from that of the Central Plains of ancient China. The Ox-tiger Table of the Warring States Period is a representative bronze ware from ancient Yunnan area. The whole item was cast in the shape of a big ox, with its four legs as the legs of the table and its back being the table top. A tiger, with its four legs gripping the ox, is biting the ox's tail. With the ox leaning forward and the tiger backward, the whole table is kept balanced. A small ox is standing leisurely under the belly of the ox, which has further enhanced the stability of the table. The design depicts that the ox is willing to sacrifice itself to the tiger, in order to protect its child. This is a comparatively large bronze ware from ancient Yunnan area, and it has naturally and vividly combined three animals together, and formed a harmonious dynamic and static combination. With ingenious structure and design, this bronze ware has combined the featurs of the four-legged table of Central Plains with and the flavors of local and minority ethnic culture of ancient Yunnan area, which makes it a masterpiece of Chinese bronze ware. Bronze shell containers of ancient Yunnan area are various in their decorative patterns, such as the patterns of horse-riding, hunting, music-playing, seeding and weaving. There are few decorative patterns in the bronze wares from the early period of time, and most of them are graphic ones. However, as ancient Yunnan area entered into Bronze Age, these graphic patterns were developed into pictorial patterns. These pictorial patterns, originating from real life, had vividly depicted the situations like farming, hunting, herding, dancing and playing music, which were the authentic records of the social life in ancient Yunnan area. Taking the Gilded Bronze Shell Container of the Western Han Dynasty as an example, this bronze container has the pattern of a man riding on the back of a horse to herd oxen. There are tiger-shaped ears on both sides of the container. And, above the cover, there is a person, who is riding a horse and is equipped with sword, standing on the top of the square stage, with four oxen surrounding the stage. This person is obviously the owner of the oxen. This is the vivid reappearance of the daily life of that time.

Beast face pattern is a popular decorative pattern on the surface of a bronze ware, commonly used from the Shang Dynasty to the early period of the Zhou Dynasty. Ancient people had combined the features of various beasts with the imaginations of them, and designed this pattern. Generally, beast face pattern is in the shape of the head of an animal, combining the features of insect, fish, bird and animal, and consists of the patterns of eye, nose, eyebrow, ear and mouth. This pattern, well structured and always with the face exaggeratedly enlarged, is full of decorative nature and is a major decorative pattern for bronze wares in ancient China. The application of beast face pattern would provide a mysterious atmosphere for us.

Except for a few bronze wares found in the Indus River Valley, most bronze wares in the world have no inscription. Inscription is a striking feature of ancient Chinese bronze wares that distinguishes them from bronze wares of other cultures. Inscription was cast on the surface of the bronze wares from the Shang Dynasty to the Period of Spring and Autumn. Since the Warring States Period and the Qin and Han Dynasties, inscription had been engraved or chiseled on the surface of the bronze wares. Most of the bronze wares in ancient China do have inscriptions, and there are over 3,000 pieces of bronze wares with inscriptions in the Shang Dynasty alone. These inscriptions have characters from several to hundreds, which are the important raw material for the research of the social life of that time.

The earliest inscription appeared in the late period of the Shang Dynasty. Inscriptions of this time only consisted of several characters, most of which were family badges, names of the people and their ancestors, such as Fuhao. Most bronze wares from the Western Zhou Dynasty inscriptions, some of which consisted of hundreds of characters, such as Maogong Tripod which has been preserved in the National Palace Museum of Taipei. This tripod is said to be excavated from Shaanxi Province in the late years of Daoguang Reign of the Qing Dynasty. There is a 32-line 499-character inscription on the inner surface of the tripod, which is the longest one by now. The inscription recorded completely Emperor Xuan's conferring of the title of nobility to Duke Mao. Some bronze wares, based on the inscriptions on them, are the standard vessels ordered to be made by emperors, such as Li Gui (a bronze food container made by Li) of the reign of Emperor Wu in the Zhou Dynasty.

Inscriptions are very important for historical research. In 1976, a Li Gui was unearthed from a pit of the Zhou Dynasty in Lintong County of Shaanxi Province. The 4-line 32-character inscription of this Li Gui mentioned the exact date of Emperor Wu attacking and quickly defeating Emperor Zhou, the last emperor of the Shang Dynasty. This inscription provided useful evidence for the division of the Shang and Zhou Dynasties, and also confirmed the history of Emperor Wu launching campaigns against Emperor Zhou, which was recorded on some ancient history books. Two years after defeating Emperor zhou, Emperor Wu of the Zhou Dynasty died , and Emperor Cheng became his successor, with Duke Zhou acting as the regent. Guanshu and Caishu, due to their resentment to the rise of Duke Zhou, colluded with the offsprings of Emperor Zhou and led an insurrection. Duke Zhou led the army by himself and spent three years ending this rebellion. This important history had been confirmed by the inscriptions on several bronze wares, such as Ranfang Tripod, Qin Gui, Square Tripod of Duke Zhou. In 1965, a bronze He Zun of the Zhou Dynasty was excavated in Baoji County of Shaanxi Province. The inscriptions on it recorded the history that Emperor Cheng, in order to defend attacks from the remaining power of the Shang Dynasty and from the minority ethnic group from the Eastern area, followed the unfulfilled wish of Emperor Wu, and established the city of Chengzhou to be the center of the country. This inscriptions and the historical records on Shangshu confirmed with each other. Some inscriptions provide a lot of information for the research of social economic development of the time. For example, the inscriptions on Wei He, Wu Si Wei Tripod and some other bronze wares have mentioned the system of land ownership. The inscription on Wu Tripod have recorded the transaction of slavers in detail. It is also an important material for the research of legal system in the Western Zhou Dynasty. Mr. Guo Moruo, wrote in the preface to Pictorial Catalogue of the Inscriptions on the Bronze Wares from the Zhou Dynasty, "It is declared that the value of one inscription on these bronze wares is equal to one article in Shangshu, however, the historical research of these inscriptions is more valuable than those literal records. "

Ⅳ. The Porspect of Chinese Bronze Ware Trading Market

With the fast development of Chinese economy and the living standard of Chinese people, antique collection has become a habit of common people in China, and has accessed to their daily life. According to some statistics in developed countries, among the people with the property over 1 million dollars, 70%~80% of them would invest in the antique market. In China, however, 3% of the people with the property over 10 million yuan would invest in the antique market. It is safe to say that the market of antique in China is still in the early stage of its development. With the further development of economy and further enhancement of people's understanding of antiques, more and more investors will enter into this market. In fact, the traders at various auctions used to be those who had family tradition of antique collection, or who were experts of this field themselves. This situation has greatly changed in the past several years. Besides those kinds of collectors and experts, there are many new faces at these auctions. There are investors in this market, and there are more speculators in it. Many presidents and chairmen of famous enterprises in China participated in the spring auctions and autumn auctions in 2010, and purchased almost all the items. During the same period, many private entrepreneurs, especially those from Jiangsu, Zhejiang, Beijing and Northeast China have become the main purchasers of the high-price works of art. Mr. Chen shoukang, the executive president of Asia Sothebys described, "These purchasers, aged from 40 to 50, are from all walks of life, especially from industries like finance, real estate, mineral and energy. Most of them are managers of successful listed companies. They have deep pockets at the auction, always aim at the items of the highest grade, and offer the highest bidding price at the auction." "These new comers at the auction amounts around 30% of all the purchasers, and some of them are upstarts with the overseas education background, successful in business like finance, real estate or hightech." Some analysts declared that this bloom of antique auction was caused by the smart and fast-moving Wenzhou (in Zhejiang) real estate investors group and the rich coal mine owners from Shanxi Province, who have entered into the market of antiques and artworks since 2010. According to the information from insiders of the industry, most of the top private entrepreneurs are so enthusiastic in these artworks, and their collections, compared with those of some museums, are larger in quantity and better in quality. At present, there are still many successful businessmen traveling all around the world to collect those treasures of artwork. And once their desirable items appear, they would not hesitate to obtain them at high prices. In the past two years, Taiyuan, the city of Shanxi Province has been favored by some major auction corporations in Chinese mainland, and has been selected as stop one for their national itinerant exhibitions.

In the first half of 2005, Zhejiang Provincial Bureau of Cultural Relics organized a team of experts to undertake the investigation on the private collection of cultural antiques within this province. The result of this investigation showed that the collection of antiques was booming in this province, and the collectors were mainly composed of private entrepreneurs, professionals and amateurs. The structure of the collectors in this province was like the structure of a pyramid. That is to say, private entrepreneurs, being the smallest group among these three kinds, invested the largest amount of money into collection; while amateurs, being the largest group among these three kinds, invested the lest amount of money in to collection. According to this investigation, there were over 40 associations and over 5,000 members in the whole province, with 2 associations in every city on average. In spite of the fact that many collectors never participate in any associations at all, the number of the members of those associations is still increasing. Bronze ware had a long history of being favored by emperors, aristocrats and wealthy businessmen in ancient time. Nowadays, bronze ware, being an artwork with a high-rate return, is going to be greatly appreciated in the future.

With the increasing number of the collectors, the need of bronze wares has also greatly increased in the market. Although there are a great number of bronze wares in China, the number of bronze wares in the circulation market is small, due to various reasons. Firstly, bronze wares are the articles produced a long time ago, and gradually become relics with the ending of the Bronze Age. The total number of the bronze wares is limited, as people after Bronze Age stopped producing bronze wares. Secondly, because of the vicissitudes of this time, all the bronze wares were buried deeply in the earth, and all the bronze wares we found today are unearthed articles in different times. The number of the bronze wares has greatly decreased, as many of them had been ruined during the process of being buried, or been ruined in the war or for other reasons, if they were unearthed in early times. Thirdly, most of the bronze wares belong to the collections of museums. A lot of museums are non-profit organizations, and their collections are not allowed to enter into the market. Finally, bronze wares are precious cultural relics in China, and are under the protection of a series of law and regulations. Trading of bronze wares is strictly controlled in China. Bronze wares that can be legally traded in the market can generally be divided into two categories: those excavated before 1949, which have detailed written records about their history of transaction; and those returned from overseas. The policy is stricter for the bronze wares to enter into the auction. Not all the bronze wares returned from overseas are allowed to be transacted at the auction, and only those excavated before 1949, and with detailed written records of transaction history since then, were able to enter into the auction. Of course, we have to notice that there are a large number of bronze wares being transacted in private, and some of the items are the newly excavated cultural relics. However, all these transactions are illegal, not protected by the law, and could never be undertaken in formal and legal transaction channels, such as auction or exhibition for antiques. Even for those bronze items that are suitable for the legal transaction, the number is far from large. It is understandable that a collector is unlikely to sell one of his favorite bronze items shortly after obtaining it. Taking Elephant-shaped Tripod of Freer Gallery of Art as an example, the donator had made his donation will that this tripod could not be away from the gallery. That is to say, this tripod, unless in some special situations, is unlikely to appeared at any auction. According to the introduction of an article, there are over 10 antique shops specialized in bronze wares in Hollywood Street and Hong Kong. The owners of these shops declared that, since 2002, most of the bronze wares with the transaction price over 10 million HKD have been bought by Mr. Cao Xingcheng . Mr. Cao is the emeritus chairman of United Microelectronics Corporation of Taiwan . Mr. Cao is also a great collector of antiques, and he is fond of Chinese bronze wares, including many precious bronze mirrors. Mr. Cao's home, displaying many treasures of bronze wares, is just like a museum. Several years ago, Mr. Cao had been honored as one of the "100 Great Collectors of Artworks". Mr. Cao's collection of bronze wares would hardly appear at the auction in the near future.

Due to all these reasons, there exists unbalance between the collectors and the collections. And this unbalance will not disappear under current Chinese policy on cultural relics. This unbalance leads to the fierce competitions among collectors, which has fully been exhibited in the competition for the Square Lei with the Inscription of Mintianquan in the spring of 2001 in the U.S.A. This Lei was unearthed in Taoyuan of Hunan Province in 1922. The item is composed of two parts, the body and the cover, and the cover is now preserved in the Hunan Provincial Museum. In order to make the two parts of this national treasure reunited, Shanghai Museum and Poly Art Museum raised a sum of money together to participate in this auction for the body of this Square Lei. However, the body of this Square Lei was obtained at last by a French buyer with the price 40% over the price offered by the Chinese buyer. The competition, in turn, will further stimulate the rise of the price. On June 3rd, 2010, a calligraphy work of Huang Tingjian (one of the most famous calligraphers in the Song Dynasty) Di Zhu Ming was auctioned at the base price of 80 million RMB. After 68 rounds of competitive bidding, this calligraphy work was sold at the hammer price of 436.8 milion RMB, which is the new record of the transaction price of Chinese artwords. This is also a good example of the high-speed rise of the price of Chinese artwords.

Once the market of the bronze ware is formed, it will be proved to be a profitable one. Encouraged by the profit, many counterfeits of bronze ware will appear in the market. The faking of bronze wares has a long history, from the Song Dynasty till now. Some of these counterfeits have some minor problems in material, shape, or decorative pattern, but some others are so nicely produced that even experts of bronze wares could not distinguish them from the real ones. Especially at present, with the application of many techniques of forgery that are never heard of, all kinds of counterfeits appear in the current market. These counterfeits are beyond our imagination, and are hard to be authenticated. If a collector wants to survive in this market, he or she will have to know the authentication at first. Successful collection is based on accurate authentication. And without this technique of authentication, it is hard to realize the maintenance and the rise of the value of bronze wares, not to mention the further research. For the bronze wares, authentication will help us to tell the true from the fake, and will also help us to understand the historical value and artistic beauty embedded in them.

I . Vessels

Bronze Tripod with Beast Face Patterns

Origin: Late Shang Dynasty
Height: 26 cm
Hammer Price: RMB 3,300,000
Name of Auction Company: Liaoning Zone
Date of Transaction: 2008-07-27

Bronze tripod has been regarded as a ritual object since the Xia Dynasty. It is recorded that, after the founding of the Xia Dynasty, Emperor Yu the Great cast nine tripods to represent the nine provinces of the whole country. Thereafter, phrase"Nine Tripods" symbolizes the sovereignty of the nation. Inscriptions on the bronze ware were found in the Shang Dynasty. This tripod, with two upright ears on the rim, a bulged belly and three column-shaped feet, is a typical bronze article of the late Shang Dynasty. The major patterns on the tripod is beast-face patterns, a typical decoration from the Shang Dynasty to the Western Zhou Dynasty. Snake patterns and flame patterns are engraved alternatively to each other below the rim.

Bronze Tripod with Cicada Patterns

Origin: Late Shang Dynasty

Height: 34 cm   Diameter: 31cm

Hammer Price: RMB 813,280

Name of Auction Company: Chongyuan International

Date of Transaction: 2006-10-05

This tripod, with a slightly converged mouth, two upright ears, a bulged belly and three column-shaped feet, is exquisite in workmanship. Cicada patterns are engraved on the belly as the major patterns, while patterns of dragon and patterns of flame are engraved alternatively below its rim. Cicada patterns first appeared during the Neolithic Age, and became a common decoration of the bronze ware from the late Shang Dynasty to the early Zhou Dynasty. Cicada, according to traditional Chinese understanding, is of the ability of rebirth and the quality of living on wind and feeding only on dew. Cicada patterns is mostly found on the tripod and jue (an ancient wine vessel with three legs and a loop handle), and is always engraved as a leaf-like slender triangle. Bronze ware with cicada patterns, probably symbolizes the healthy and simple food and drink.

Bronze Lobed Tripod with Beast Face Patterns

Origin: Late Shang Dynasty

Height: 21.5 cm

Hammer Price: RMB 1,232,000

Name of Auction Company: Liaoning International

Date of Transaction: 2008-06-22

Lobed tripod, also known as Li Tripod, is a mixture of li (an ancient cooking tripod with hollow feet) and tripod. This tripod has two upright ears on the rim, a separatedcrotch and three cylindrical feet. This tripod has three edges according to its three feet, with beastface patterns on each side. Cylindrical feet are decorated with patterns of delicate design and thick matrix. Inscription of one word is engraved inside the tripod, which, according to the custom of the Shang Dynasty, should be a clan badge.

Bronze Quadrate Pot with Bird-shaped Flat Feet

Origin: Late Shang Dynasty

Height: 23 cm

Hammer Price: RMB 2,152,800

Name of Auction Company: Chongyuan International

Date of Transaction: 2006-10-05

Tripod (including quadrate pot) is a major category of bronze ritual objects, which represents the grade and power of the ruling class. Flat feet tripod first appeared in the early Shang Dynasty. In 1982, one quadrate pot with four phoenix-shaped feet and cloud-and-thunder patterns was excavated in Zhengzhou, Henan Province. The flat feet of the tripod in the late Shang Dynasty were always taken the shape of dragon, tiger or phoenix. This quadrate pot has two ears, a square-shaped lip, a shallow belly, a round bottom and four bird-shaped flat feet. With heads upward, and with the talons as the holder of the belly, long and deflexed tails as the stands, the whole birds are slightly outward-dipping, in order to enhance the stability of the pot. The birds, with round beaks, projecting eyes and back-curving wings, are of great craftsmanship.

Bronze Tripod with BeastFace atterns

Origin: Western Zhou Dynasty

Height: 43 cm   Diameter: 34cm

Hammer Price: RMB 4,657,500

Name of Auction Company: Chongyuan International

Date of Transaction: 2008-04-12

This tripod has a square-shaped rim, two upright ears, a bulged belly and three slightly retracting hoof-shaped feet. Tiger-face patterns and inverted dragon patterns are found below the rim. beast face patterns are also found on the upper area of the feet. The tripod, with its big size, fine casting, natural and unfretted design, is full of the features of the craftsmanship in the early Western Zhou Dynasty. The inscriptions of "precious wine vessel made by the Duke of E Area" are engraved inside the tripod. Bronze wares from E area have been excavated since a long time ago. According to the inscriptions in the Tripod of Duke Yu Fang in E Area, Duke Yu Fang once presented gifts to and feasted Emperor Zhou, and was granted reward by the Emperor. In November 2007, archeologists of Suizhou City explored and sorted out a tomb of the early Western Zhou Dynasty in Yangzishan Area, and a large number of precious bronze wares were excavated. The excavated bronze wares, altogether 27 items, include rectangular pots, round pots, etc., most of which have inscriptions engraved on. Judging from the shape and structure of the tomb, features of the excavated articles and the content of the inscriptions, this tomb should belong to the Duke of E Area in the early Western Zhou Dynasty. This tripod, based on its shape and the engraving of the inscriptions, should also belong to Duke of Western E Area, which shows the great value of the article.

Bronze Rectangular Pot with Beast Face Patterns

Origin: Western Zhou Dynasty

Height: 25.7 cm

Hammer Price: RMB 1,029,500

Name of Auction Company: Chongyuan International

Date of Transaction: 2006-05-02

Rectangular pot was popular in the time period from the Shang Dynasty to Western Zhou Dynasty. According to the archaeological records, rectangular pots were mainly excavated from the tombs of higher nobilities. This pot, with an up-right mouth, a folded rim and two massive ears, has an unbent rectangle belly supported by four column-shaped feet. There are edges on the corners of the square belly, with the decoration of beast face patterns engraved in relief on the surface. Delicate cloud-and-thunder patterns are engraved as a contrast to the beast face patterns. The upper parts of the feet are decorated with triangular cloud patterns, and the bottom of the belly is decorated with grid patterns in thin lines. The beast face patterns in this pot are of exquisite craftsmanship, and vividly present the mysterious and ferocious feelings of the beast.

Bronze Tripod with Curling-up Dragon Patterns

Origin: Spring and Autumn Period
Height: 38 cm
Hammer Price: RMB 313,200
Name of Auction Company: Chongyuan International
Date of Transaction: 2008-07-26

This tripod has square-shaped rim, straight neck, deep belly, round bottom and hoof-shaped feet. Hoof-shaped feet first appeared in the Western Zhou Dynasty, and became the mainstream in the Eastern Zhou Dynasty. Generally speaking, upright ears were most likely found in the tripods of the Western Zhou Dynasty; while side ears in those of the Eastern Zhou Dynasty. This tripod is an article from the Eastern Zhou Dynasty. Dragon patterns are engraved on the neck, belly and ears of the tripod. The dragons, winding in body, are decorated with neatly arranged spot patterns. The beast face patterns are also engraved in relief on the upper parts of the foot, with the central ridge projecting out.

Bronze Tripod with Curling-up Snake Patterns

Origin: Warring States Period

Height: 24 cm   Width: 32 cm

Hammer Price: RMB 326,040

Name of Auction Company: Hong Kong Sino Art

Date of Transaction: 2006-11-25

Tripod used to be cooking utensil. Equipped with long feet, it can be heated beneath. With the function as cooking utensil fading away and the function as ritual object enhanced, tripod with short feet came into exist in the Warring States Period, and became very popular in the Han Dynasty. This tripod, with slightly a retracting mouth, two side ears and three short feet, has a round and bulged-out cover, attached with a ring-shaped knob. The tripod is decorated with curling-up snake patterns. Curling-up snake patterns, also called curling-up dragon patterns, is popular in the Spring and Autumn Period, with the head of snake taking the shape of triangle and the eyes projecting out.

Bronze Li with BeastFace Patterns

Origin: Late Shang Dynasty
Height: 23.1 cm
Hammer Price: RMB 2,016,000
Name of Auction Company: Beijing Zhongjia
Date of Transaction: 2010-05-09

Li is a cooking utensil in ancient times. According to Erya, "tripod…with decoration of feet is called li". Or, according to the History of Han Dynasty, "tripod with hollow feet is called li". This li, with two upright ears on the rim and three pouched feet, is engraved with beast face patterns as its major decorative patterns on the belly. Kui (a one-body-and-one-foot dragon in Chinese mythology) patterns and vortex patterns are also found on the neck of this item. The whole item, in shining patina green color, is unique in design and patterns.

Bronze Yan with Beast-Face Patterns

Origin: Western Zhou Dynasty
Height: 39 cm
Hammer Price: RMB 495,000
Name of Auction Company: Shanghai Chongyuan
Date of Transaction: 2006-08-13

Yan is the steaming cauldron in ancient China. Yan consists of zeng in the upper part and li in the lower part, with a pierced grate to connect each other. In the process of cooking, rice is placed in zeng, and water is put into li. After heating li, steam will evaporate through the grate to braise the rice. This yan, with a wide-flared mouth and two upright ears, has a grate to connect zeng and li. The rim is decorated with heavy-lined beast face patterns, and the belly is decorated with triangle-shaped beast face patterns. The li is decorated with ox-shaped patterns. The whole article, grandiose in structure, has combined the originality of its patterns and the delicacy of its engraving.

Bronze Yan with Patternss of Intertwining Dragons

Origin: Spring and Autumn Period

Height: 32.5 cm

Diameter: 29 cm

Hammer Price: RMB 110,032

Name of Auction Company: Chongyuan International

Date of Transaction: 2006-10-05

These two yans are of the similar size and design. The zeng, in the upper part, has a wide-flared mouth, a folded rim and a convergent neck. The shoulder is formed by the projecting ridge that connects the neck and the belly, with a flexible ring on each side. With a flat bottom, the belly of the zeng is slantingly convergent. There are three circles of intertwining dragon patterns to decorate the belly of zeng. Li, with an upright mouth, a round shoulder and a bulged belly, has three pouched feet. There are two knobs on the shoulder of the li, and a projecting ridge on the belly. Although the zeng is comparatively big, the whole article appears stable, due to the round belly and the three short feet of the li.

Bronze Gui with Beast Face Patterns

Origin: Late Shang Dynasty
Height: 16.5 cm   Diameter: 26 cm
Hammer Price: RMB 417,600
Name of Auction Company: Chongyuan International
Date of Transaction: 2008-07-26

Gui, a food vessel in ancient China, first appeared in the Shang Dynasty, and still existed till the Warring States Period. It is recorded in the Rites of Zhou, that "gui will be applied in the sacrificial ceremony". According to the Book of Rites and the archeological discovery, gui always appears in pairs, and is always accompanied with tripod. For example, we can find 4 guis accompanied with 5 tripods, or 6 guis with 7 tripods, with the larger number representing higher ranking of social status. This gui, with wide-flared mouth, round bottom and round feet, has two beast-shaped ears on the flanks of the slightly bulged belly. Beast heads are engraved in relief below the rim, with beast face patterns on both sides. Gui is various in design, and this one falls into one of the important categories.

Bronze Gui with Beast Face Patterns

Origin: Western Zhou Dynasty
Height: 14 cm
Hammer Price: RMB 1,357,200
Name of Auction Company: Chongyuan International
Date of Transaction: 2008-07-26

Gui, a food vessel, has experienced various changes through its development. Gui of the Shang Dynasty, round shaped, has a wide-flared mouth, a deep belly, round feet and two ears or no ears. Gui of this time is decorated with beast face patterns, and the ears of some guis might take the shape of beast head. In the Western Zhou Dynasty, besides previously existed design, a lot of newly designed guis appeared, such as four-eared gui, four-footed gui and gui of round body and square stand etc. And some guis were equipped with covers; guis of the Shang and Zhou Dynasties might have massive and heavy structure, and were decorated with the patterns of beast face, cloud and thunder, nipples, etc. Only a few guis had no decorative patterns, or just one or two bow-string patterns; guis of the Spring and Autumn Period became thin in its base, with the cover taking the shape of lotus leaves. Gui became rare after the Warring States Period. This gui, with a wide-flared mouth and an upright belly, has two ears on both sides of its belly and is shaped of a beasthead and a birdbody. The belly is decorated with beast face patterns, and the round feet are decorated with dragon patterns.

Gold Dotted Bronze Gui with Beast Face Patterns

Origin: Qing Dynasty(17 th)
Height: 24.2 cm
Hammer Price: RMB 436,800
Name of Auction Company: Hong Kong Sotheby's
Date of Transaction: 2006-04-10

Gold dotting is the decoration technology which means gold spots or patches are dotted on the undercoat and are recoated with lacquer. This bronze gui, with a wide-flared mouth, a bulged belly and a round foot, is decorated with beast face patterns and gold dotting. Dotted gold, various in size and high in fineness, makes the whole article shining and elegant. And the oxygenation of some parts provides the article a primitive and unsophisticated beauty. Combining the structure and the decorative patterns of the Western Zhou Dynasty and the technology of gold dotting, this article is one of the masterpieces of bronze wares of the Qing Dynasty.

Bronze Xu with Double-ring Patterns

Origin: Western Zhou Dynasty
Height: 18 cm
Hammer Price: RMB 753,480
Name of Auction Company: Chongyuan International
Date of Transaction: 2006-10-05

Xu is an ancient vessel to hold glutinous millet, rice and sorghum. Archeological discovery shows that Xu, besides the function of holding food, can be used to simmer. The whole article is similar to gui in shape except its rounded rectangular shape. Xu first appeared in the mid-Western Zhou Dynasty, prevailed in the late Western Zhou Dynasty and gradually disappeared in the Spring and Autumn Period. This Xu, oval-shaped, has a slightly convergent mouth, a slightly bulged belly and a beast-head-shaped ear on each side. There are door-shaped holes in its round feet. The cover is bulged out and attached with two upright door-shaped knobs, which can be used as holders. The belly and cover are decorated with beasteye patterns, and the rim is decorated with double-ring patterns. There are inscriptions engraved on the inside of the cover and belly.

Bronze Fu with Dragon Patterns

Origin: Spring and Autumn Period

Height: 16 cm   Length: 28.5 cm   Width: 16.5 cm

Hammer Price: RMB 167,440

Name of Auction Company: Chongyuan International

Date of Transaction: 2006-10-05

Fu is a square grain receptacle used at sacrificial ceremonies in ancient times. The basic shape of fu is rectangular, with cover and holder same in size and symmetrical in design. Fu first appeared in the early Western Zhou Dynasty, prevailed in the time periods from the late Western Zhou Dynasty to the early Spring and Autumn Period and disappeared in the late Warring States Period. This fu, rectangular in shape, has a wide-flared mouth, four outward square feet, and four half-ring-shaped ears on the short sides both of cover and holder.

Bronze Dou with Worm Patterns

Origin: Warring States Period
Height: 21 cm
Hammer Price: RMB 199,784
Name of Auction Company: Hong Kong Sino Art
Date of Transaction: 2008-07-26

Dou is a food vessel to hold the meat paste, seasoning or millet. The bronze dou was evolved from the pottery item which first appeared in the Shang Dhynasty, then was popularly used in the Zhou Dynasty, and went to its boom time in the late Spring and Autumn Period and the Warring States Period. This dou has an inward mouth, a ring-shaped knob, a deep belly, a horn-shaped foot and a cover with a round hand grab. It is decorated with exquisite worm patterns and has a stable and graceful sense.

Bronze Kettle with Beast Patterns

Origin: Late Zhou Dynasty
Height: 27.5 cm
Hammer Price: RMB 3,106,000
Name of Auction Company: Chongyuan International
Date of Transaction: 2008-04-12

Bronze kettle appeared from the late Zhou Dynasty, and then eventually became rare in the Han Dynasty. This kettle has a small mouth, a long neck, a plump belly and a round foot. It has a lid with a mouth and a round handle with knob on the side of its belly. The handle is decorated with rhombus patterns with two beast heads on the end. The surface of the lid, the belly and the foot are decorated with beast face patterns. It has smooth lines and beautiful decorative patterns, with high value of craftsmanship.

Bronze Kettle with Wave Patterns

Origin: Western Zhou Dynasty

Height: 56 cm   Belly Diameter: 31 cm

Hammer Price: RMB 4,186,000

Name of Auction Company: Chongyuan International

Date of Transaction: 2006-10-05

    This item has an open mouth, a long neck, a plump belly and a round foot. It has a lid with an outward mouth. On the neck, there are two beast-shaped ears with rings on it. The lid top and the foot are decorated with scale patterns. The lower part of the lid and the joint part of the neck and belly are decorated with beast patterns. The rings and the ears are decorated with triangle patterns. The main part of the neck and the belly are decorated with broad wave patterns. By close observation, you can find an almost invisible dragon. These kinds of dragon transformation patterns were very popular patterns in the middle and late Zhou Dynasty.

Bronze Kettle with Beast Face Patterns

Origin: Western Zhou Dynasty

Height: 33 cm

Hammer Price: RMB 828,920

Name of Auction Company: Chongyuan International

Date of Transaction: 2006-05-02

This item is shaped in oval, with an open mouth, a long neck, a downward plump belly and a round foot. On its neck, there is a round ear on two sides which is linked with the handle. It has a lid with a small mouth. The handle is decorated with dragon patterns, and the neck and lid are decorated with beast patterns. Several bars separate the belly into 8 parts without decoration. It has the inscriptions of "Cuofuyi" on the inner lid which tell us that a man named Cuo made this item as a sacrificial vessel to his father Fuyi.

Bronze Square Kettle with Beast Ears (one pair)

Origin: Spring and Autumn Period
Height: 33.5 cm
Hammer Price: RMB 253,000
Name of Auction Company: Hong Kong Sino Art
Date of Transaction: 2007-05-05

Kettle is an ancient wine or water vessel. These two kettles have the same modeling, and should be produced by the same workshop. They both have a shrink neck, a plump belly, a square foot and a spuare lid. The two sides each has a beast handle with rings on it. With three bow-string patterns and a vertical line, the whole surface of the belly is divided into 8 parts.

Bronze Gourd Bottle with Bird Lid

Origin: Spring and Autumn Period
Height: 31.7 cm
Hammer Price: RMB 486,000
Name of Auction Company: Germany Nagel
Date of Transaction: 2005-11-14

This bronze bottle is shaped as gourd, with a short round foot and a moveable handle on the belly. The handle has a chain to link with the lid. The lid is shaped as a bird, with a knob to tie the chain. The body has several decorative bars around it. This bronze ware is simulated in the gourd shape, which appeared in the Western Zhou Dynasty and became popular in the Eastern Zhou Dynasty.

Flat Bronze Kettle with Inlaid Snake Patterns

Origin: Warring States Period
Height: 36 cm
Hammer Price: RMB 334,880
Name of Auction Company: Chongyuan International
Date of Transaction: 2006-10-05

This item has a small mouth, a flat round belly and a square foot. On its shoulder, it is decorated with a beast head with a ring. It has a lid with beast knobs on it. On its belly, there are irregular squares composed by vertical and horizontal bars. Inside the squares, it is decorated with overlapped feather-like bumps and delicate snake patterns. The triangle part on the neck and the grid on the belly are decorated with inlaid red copper. This kind of Kettle was the newly produced wine vessel in the Warring States Period.

Flat Bronze Kettle with Beast Face Patterns and Inlaid Gold and Silver

Origin: Warring States Period

Height: 26.5 cm   width: 25.5 cm

Transaction Hammer Price: RMB 858,000

Name of Auction Company: Liaoning International

Date of Transaction: 2006-10-29

The item has a small mouth, a flat round belly and a square foot. On its shoulder, it is decorated with a beast head with a ring. On its belly, there are irregular squares composed by vertical and horizontal bars. Inside the square, it is decorated with hornless dragon. The inlaid gold and silver is a newly developed craftsmanship after the Eastern Zhou Dynasty. This item has complicate and exquisite decorative patterns, demonstrating the highly developed workmanship.

Square Bronze Kettle with Geometric Patterns

Origin: Warring States Period
Height: 36 cm
Hammer Price: RMB 3,109,600
Name of Auction Company: Chongyuan International
Date of Transaction: 2006-10-05

This item has a square mouth, a straight neck, a curve shoulder, a plump belly and a round foot. Two sides are decorated with a beast head with a ring. The whole body has geometric decorative patterns filled with turquoise and red copper. All the inlaid ornaments are kept very well. The producer used the different colors of turquoise and red copper to make the decorative patterns have noble and elegant effects. It is a perfect example for the inlaying workmanship.

Bronze Kettle with Hunting Patterns

Origin: Warring States Period
Height: 37 cm
Hammer Price: RMB 1,680,000
Name of Auction Company: International Auction of China
Date of Transaction: 2010-06-19

    This item has an open mouth, a shrink neck, a round shoulder, a plump belly and a straight-standing round foot. All its body is carved with decoration patterns, which can be divided into six parts. Its neck is decorated with patterns which shows that a bird is eating a dragon and beasts are fighting for the sun. The shoulder is decorated with beast patterns which is abstract and graceful. The main decorative patterns on the shoulder and belly are the hunting scenery. The people in the scenery hold the shields or the swords to defend or attack, or take the spears to stab, or assemble up and carry the bow and arrow to shoot. The dragons, rhinos, wolves and birds are escaping or fighting back. Between the lower part of the belly and the foot, it is decorated with the patterns of birdmen and birds eating snakes. The foot is a high-standing round foot which is decorated with fret and geometric patterns. This item originally has paint filled in the decorative patterns to highlight the lines. As time passed by, the paint fell off, only leaving the ancient bronze ground color to demonstrate the fine workmanship.

Square Bronze Kettle with Beast Face Patterns

Origin: Qing Dynasty
Height: 46 cm
Hammer Price: RMB 896,000
Name of Auction Company: Sungari International
Date of Transaction: 2006-06-07

This kettle has a square mouth, a straight neck, a long and plump belly and a round foot. On the two sides of its neck are a pair of beast head handles with two rings. The neck and the lower part of the belly are decorated with beast patterns. On the bottom, it is inscribed with 4 regular Chinese characters: Chunhuaqiushi (spring blossoms and autumn fruits). This kettle was imitated from the bronze ware in the Spring and Autumn Period, which followed the established modeling, exquisite patterns and fine workmanship. From the honorable manner of the royal palace it demonstrates to us, it is a product from the royal workshop.

Fujizuxin Bronze Zun

Origin: Late Zhou Dynasty

Height: 34 cm   Mouth Diameter: 24 cm

Hammer Price: RMB 5,500,000

Name of Auction Company: Shanghai Chongyuan

Date of Transaction: 2004-07-03

This zun is an ancient wine vessel, with an open mouth, a long neck, a plump belly and a high round foot. Between the lower part of its neck and the foot, it has four extruded edges. The whole body is decorated with different beast and bird patterns. On the inner side of the foot, it is inscribed with four Chinese characters: Fujizuxin. It shows that this zun was made as a sacrificial object dedicated to Fuji and Zuxin. This zun demonstrates the high standard and exquisite workmanship of Chinese bronzewares.

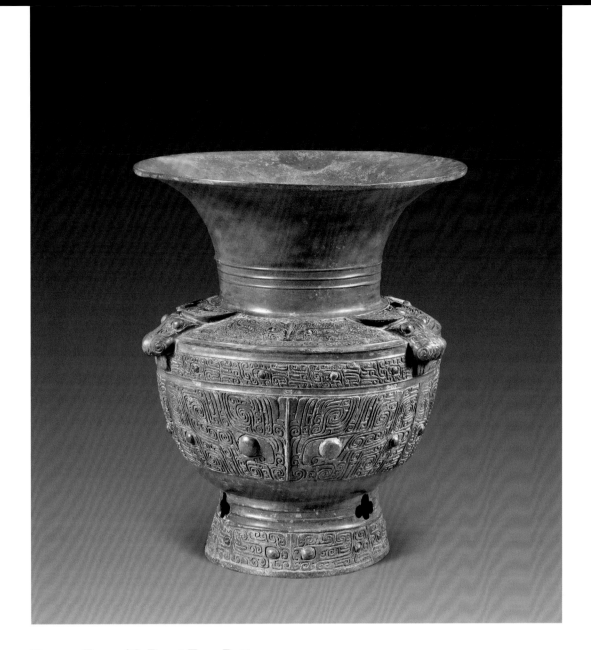

Bronze Zun with Beast Face Patterns

Origin: Shang Dynasty
Height: 36.4 cm
Hammer Price: RMB 6,944,000
Name of Auction Company: Sungari International
Date of Transaction: 2007-08-20

    This zun has an open mouth, a long neck, a fold broad shoulder, a round foot and a downward contracted belly. It is decorated with three buffalo heads, thus it is also named as "Zun with Taotie Patterns and Three Buffalo Heads". On its neck, it is carved with three bow-string patterns. On the upper part of its foot, it has three cross-shaped holes and two bow-string decoration. This zun, used to be collected by Sengoku family, a Japanese entrepreneur, was exhibited with Zilong Tripod at Osaka, Japan and an exhibition catalog named as "The Antique Pithy of Chinese Dynasties" was published.

Bronze Phoenix Zun

Origin: Western Zhou Dynasty

Height: 30 cm   Length: 32 cm

Hammer Price: RMB 3,348,800

Name of Auction Company: Chongyuan International

Date of Transaction: 2006-10-05

This zun is shaped as a phoenix, with a dragon head, two dragon horns, a broad mouth and exposed buckteeth. It has a plump body, two twisted wings, a broad-curved tail, and two duck-like claws. On its back, there are a small standing bird and a tiger. The phoenix's chest and tail are decorated with a dragon with its head looking back. The mouth of the tiger on the chest has an open hollow as this vessel's mouth. This phoenix zun is the only one with such modeling in the bronze wares.

Bronze Zun with Beast Face Patterns

Origin: Western Zhou Dynasty

Height: 30 cm

Hammer Price: RMB 792,000

Name of Auction Company: China Guardian

Date of Transaction: 2006-06-03

This zun has an open mouth, a slight broader belly and a round foot. On its neck, belly and foot, there are four raised edges. It is decorated with banana leaf, cicada, silkworm, beast and cloud-and-thunder patterns. On its foot, it is inscribed with four chinese characters. It used to have a rosewood stand inscribed with four chinese characters:Qian long yu wan (Emperor Qianlong's rare curiosa).

Square Bronze Zun with Gilding Dragon Patterns

Origin: Reign of Emperor Qianlong,Qing Dynasty
Height: 49.5 cm
Hammer Price: RMB 1,535,250
Name of Auction Company: Chieftown Auction
Date of Transaction: 2008-05-28

Zun is a wine vessel. This zun has a square body, an open mouth, a constricted belly and a round foot. Its front is carved with a dragon and an inscribed Chinese character "Shou" (longevity) on head. Its middle part is also decorated with longevity inscriptions. All its body is gilded. This zun was specially made by the royal workshop to celebrate Emperor Qianlong's birthday.

Bronze Goblet in the Shape of a Sacrificial Animal with Embedded Filamentary Silver

Origin: Ming and Qing Dynasties
Height: 19.4 cm
Hammer Price: RMB 524,160
Name of Auction Company: Hong Kong Christie's
Date of Transaction: 2006-05-30

Goblet is the wine vessel used as a ritual object. Ox of a uniform color was used as a sacrificial animal at ancestral temples in ancient times. This goblet is in the shape of an sacrificial ox. Goblet could also be shaped like other animals, such as birds. Goblets in the shape of a sacrificial animal were very popular in the Shang and Zhou Dynasties, but became rare in the Spring and Autumn Period. This goblet, with the ox standing straightly and its tail hanging curled, has a cover and a mouth on its back. There is embedded filamentary silver to decorate the neck of the ox. The whole article, with fine design and delicate decoration, fully embodies the high craftsmanship of bronze manufacture.

Bronze"Wei Fu" You with Inscription

Origin: Late Shang Dynasty
Height: 33.2 cm
Hammer Price: RMB 1,540,000
Name of Auction Company: Shanghai Chongyuan
Date of Transaction: 2005-06-29

You is a wine vessel in ancient times. This you, with an oval-shaped body, a convergent mouth, a bulged-out belly and a round foot, has a cover and a round knob. The loop handle is connected with two semi-circular knobs on both sides of the belly. The knobs are goat-head-shaped and have two long and round horns. The cover and the neck of this you are decorated with dragon patterns, and there is a small and delicate bronze statue of goathead in the central part of the neck. There are inscriptions, which mean "made by Master Wei Fu", on the inner surface of the belly and the cover. This you once belonged to Mr. Luo Zhenyu (1866-1940), a famous modern epigraphist and antique collector, and is recorded in Mr. Luo's Collection of Bronze Inscriptions from the Three Dynasties (Volume 13, You, the second part).

Bronze You with Beast Face Patterns

Origin: Late Shang Dynasty
Height: 30.5 cm
Hammer Price: RMB 4,657,500
Name of Auction Company: Chongyuan International
Date of Transaction: 2008-04-12

This you has an elliptic body and a round foot, with its belly bulged out. The loop handle of the you is connected, on both ends, with the two ring-shaped knobs on both sides of the rim. This you has an upright double lip mouth, with the arc-shaped cover attached with a mushroom-shaped knob. There are four edges crossing the cover, the belly and the feet. The cover and the belly are decorated with beast face patterns, and the neck is decorated with a small beast head in relief. This you has no beasthead on both ends of its handle, which is very unique for this kind of bronze ware.

Bronze You with Beast Face Patterns

Origin: Western Zhou Dynasty
Height: 23.5 cm
Hammer Price: RMB 2,376,000
Name of Auction Company: Germany Nagel
Date of Transaction: 2005-11-14

You is a wine vessel in ancient times. According to the records of ancient documents and bronze inscriptions, "Yiyou" refers to one kind of fragrant wine used in the sacrificial ceremony. You, therefore, is the vessel for this kind of wine. Mostly, you is equipped with cover, to keep the fragrance of the wine from emitting out. This you, with an elliptic body and a double-lip mouth, has two small bronze oxheads on both ends of the handle. There are beast face patterns on the cover and the belly, with an edge as the central line of the patterns.

Bronze You with Bird Patterns

Origin: Ming Dynasty
Height: 24 cm
Hammer Price: RMB 253,000
Name of Auction Company: Yunnan Diancang
Date of Transaction: 2004-05-30

With a short and upright neck, bulged-out belly and heightened round foot, this you takes the shape of an ellipsoid. The high-necked cover is latched with the belly through a doublelip mouth. There is a bud-shaped knob in the middle of the cover's surface. The loop handle is decorated with ox-shaped statues on its both ends. And the loop handle is in shape of beast heads. The whole body and the cover are decorated with separated bird patterns. Bronze you first appeared in the Shang and Zhou Dynasties, and became rare after the Western Zhou Dynasty. However, bronze you resurged after the Song Dynasty.

Bronze You with Beast Face Patterns

Origin: Qing Dynasty
Height: 28 cm
Hammer Price: RMB 154,000
Name of Auction Company: Yunnan Diancang
Date of Transaction: 2004-05-30

This you, elliptic in shape, has an upright mouth, a bulged belly and a round foot. On both sides of the neck, there are short and projecting bars to hold both ends of the handle. Cover of this you is in shape of arc, with a knob in its center area. Four edges are decorating the cover and the belly, and the beast face patterns are the major decoration of this you. Compared with those of the Shang Dynasty, the decorative patterns of this you are less orderly organized, and the lines of which are less smooth and less powerful. During the time of the Qing Dynasty, the royal court paid great attention to the manufacture of the ritual articles, so were the scholar-bureaucrat and the aristocracy of the time.

Bronze He with Dragon Patterns

Origin: Western Zhou Dynasty
Height: 21.9 cm   Length: 14.5 cm
Hammer Price: RMB 209,000
Name of Auction Company: Shanghai Chongyuan
Date of Transaction: 2003-10-25

He was used for mixing and heating liquor in ancient China. According to the inscriptions of Jiliangfuhe, the word "he" is like someone taking a wheat-straw to drink liquor. Most of the hes are round in shape, having a big belly, a cover and three or four feet. And most of them have a spout in front and a handle behind. He was first discovered in Erlitou Cultural Relics (from around 2000BC to 1500BC), and was very popular in the late Shang Dynasty and early Zhou Dynasty. In the time period of Spring and Autumn, there came the he with loop handle. This he has a pouched belly, a convergent neck and three pillar feet, with the rim bending outward. The handle is in the shape of beast head, the neck is decorated with dragon patterns, and the spout is decorated with cloud patterns. There are seven Chinese characters inscribed inside the belly.

Bronze Bu with Beast Face Patterns

Origin: Late Shang Dynasty
Height: 17.5 cm   Diameter: 24 cm
Hammer Price: RMB 141,024
Name of Auction Company: Hong Kong Sino Art
Date of Transaction: 2006-07-29

Bu is used for holding wine or water. According to Yan Shigu's explanation in the History of Han Dynasty,"Bu is small jar". This bu has a contracted mouth, broad shoulders, and a ring foot with square openings. beast face patterns, as the major decorative patterns, can be found in the belly, and patterns of other styles can be found on the shoulder and the ring foot. The biggest bronze bu ever unearthed was discovered in Ningxiang County of Hunan Province, with the height of 62.5cm, diameter of mouth 57-58cm, diameter of belly 86-89cm and diameter of ring foot 55.6cm. Square opening on the ring foot is the common characteristic of bronze bu.

Bronze Bu with Beast Face Patterns

Origin: Late Shang Dynasty
Height: 43 cm
Hammer Price: RMB 28,980,000
Name of Auction Company: Chongyuan International
Date of Transaction: 2008-04-12

The round cover of this bu, being short, is perfectly integrated with the round belly. The ring foot are curled outward. There are six edges crossing the cover, belly and the foot. The cover is decorated with converted beast face patterns, with a winding-dragon-shaped knob in the middle. Three bronze beast heads are set on the shoulder, with the patterns of dragon in between. The belly is decorated with beast face patterns, while the ring foot is decorated with dragon patterns.

Bronze Lei with Flame Patterns

Origin: Late Shang Dynasty

Height: 35 cm

Hammer Price: RMB 461,600

Name of Auction Company: Chongyuan International

Date of Transaction: 2008-07-25

Lei is an vessel to hold water or wine. Records from some ancient Chinese classics confirmed these two functions of lei. It is recorded in the Book of Songs that "I will just fill your lei with wine". It is also recorded in a book about etiquettes that "Si-kong (an official title) put the water into lei, and set the lei to the east side of the washer". Lei can be divided into two groups: square lei and round lei. This lei, round in shape, has an upright mouth, a contracted neck, round shoulders, a deep and arc-shaped belly, and a flat bottom. A pair of beast-shaped ears are located on the shoulder, and a small handle is located on each side of the belly. Area around the neck is decorated with flame patterns. The neck and the belly are connected by a groove. Most of the leis have a wide-flared mouth, while this one has an upright mouth.

Square Bronze Yi with Beast Face Patterns

Origin: Late Shang Dynasty
Height: 18 cm
Hammer Price: RMB 3,348,800
Name of Auction Company: Chongyuan International
Date of Transaction: 2006-10-05

Yi is an ancient wine vessel, and is generally referred as one of the common ritual objects used in the ancestral temple. Square yi was officially named in the Song Dynasty, and was popularly used from the late Shang Dynasty to the mid-Western Zhou Dynasty. This kind of objects, cuboid in shape, have a cover, an upright mouth, a vertical belly and a ring foot. The cover, with the bottom larger than the top, is in the shape of a slope roof. There is a square opening on each side of the ring foot. The cover is decorated with inverted and separated beast face patterns, while the belly with tiger-head-shaped patterns. The rim and the ring foot are decorated with dragon patterns, but in different styles. This yi, grandiose and exquisite, fully exhibites the craftsmanship of the bronze manufacture of the time.

Bronze Gong with Beast Face Patterns

Origin: Song Dynasty

Height: 16 cm

Hammer Price: RMB 671,000

Name of Auction Company: Yunnan Diancang

Date of Transaction: 2004-05-30

Sigong is an ancient wine vessel, which is always made of horns of female rhinoceros, and was very popular in the Shang and Western Zhou Dynasties. Sentences like "I will just fill your sigong up" are found in the Book of Songs. Ouyang Xiu, a famous essayist in the Song Dynasty, wrote in his The Roadside Hut of the Old Drunkard that "when someone wins a game of cottabus or chess, when they mark up their scores in drinking games with their gongs together, or raise a cheerful din sitting or standing, it can be seen that the guests are enjoying themselves". This gong, square-shaped, has ring foot, a spout and handle. With the dragon patterns as its major decoration, this article is decorated with cloud-and-thunder patterns all around the body. Because of the fondness of the ruling class, a lot of bronze wares imitating ancient styles were produced in the Song Dynasty. This gong is one of those imitations.

Bronze Vase with Dragon-in-sea-water Patterns

Origin: Qing Dynasty
Height: 65 cm
Hammer Price: RMB 15,702,400
Name of Auction Company:
Beijing Hanhai
Date of Transaction: 2007-12-17

Vase is the vessel for wine or water. This vase has a dish-shaped mouth, an upright neck, a round shoulder and a contracted belly, with an out-turned ring foot. The whole article is decorated with dragon-in-sea-water patterns, with the dragon being in the central area of the belly, vivid and vigorous. The neck is decorated with double bow-string patterns, and the ring foot with banana leaves which form a circle around the foot. The standard inscriptions of "made in the Yongzheng Era of the Qing Dynasty"is marked on the foot. With the development of craftsmanship and technology in the Ming and Qing Dynasties, especially during the prosperous reigns of Emperor Kangxi and Qianlong, the manufacture of bronze ware had reached a new level. This vase, made of fine material, is designed vividly and delicately. Some visitors think the material of this vase is the same as those of bronze ware s of animal heads recently retrieved, and think this vase used to be held in the Yuanmingyuan Garden, which still need to be verified.

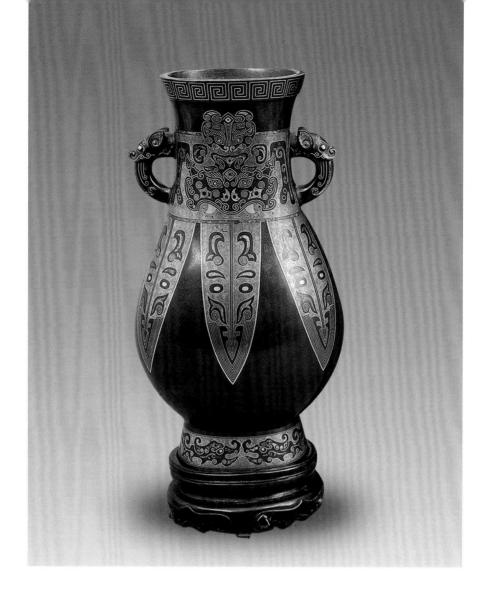

Gold-and-silver-inlaid Bronze Vase with Double Ears

Origin: Qing Dynasty

Height: 16.5 cm

Hammer Price: RMB 231,000

Name of Auction Company: Beijing Poly

Date of Transaction: 2007-06-02

This vase is made of fine and glossy brass. The patterns on the vase, being imitations of ancient bronze ware, are complicated and magnificent. There are threads of gold and silver inlaid on the surface of the vase.

Square Bronze Vase with the Patternss of Dragon and Phoenix (one pair)

Origin: Reign of Emperor Qianlong,Qing Dynasty

Height: 42.7 cm

Hammer Price: RMB 11,303,500

Name of Auction Company: Hong Kong Sotheby's

Date of Transaction: 2007-10-09

This pair of square vases, with the same model and structure, both have an upright mouth, a contracted neck, folded shoulders, and a ring foot. The ears are joined with flexible rings. These two vases, with one's major patterns being dragon and the other's being phoenix, express the extremely good fortune brought by dragon and phoenix. In traditional Chinese auspicious pictures, dragon and phoenix occupy half of the image respectively, and look at each other. At the same time, dragon and phoenix symbolize emperor and empress. On the rim of the dragon patterns vase, there are engraved words like "CAPTURE OF OHNESE PALAOE. PEKN.1860", which mean this pair of vase used to be placed in the Yuanmingyuan Garden (Imperial Garden), and was plundered in 1860.

Bronze Jia with Beast Face Patterns and Pouched Legs

Origin: Late Shang Dynasty

Height: 32.5 cm

Hammer Price: RMB 896,000

Name of Auction Company: Liaoning International

Date of Transaction: 2008-06-22

Jia is an ancient vessel for heating wine. This jia, has a wide-flared mouth, with a thickened rim. There are two upright columns on the rim, the top of which is mushroom-shaped and decorated with symmetrical rectangular spiral patterns. With the neck contracted, the belly of this jia is divided into three parts, and forms three legs. A beast-head-shaped handle is located on one side of the object. Both the neck and the belly are decorated with beast face patterns, with the nose of the beast on the belly opposite to the joint of the tails of the beasts on the neck. This article, with ingenious design and the coordination of each part, is one of the masterpieces of bronze wares.

Bronze Owl-shaped Jia

Origin: Late Shang Dynasty
Height: 25 cm
Hammer Price: RMB 2,750,800
Name of Auction Company: Chongyuan International
Date of Transaction: 2006-10-05

This jia is in shape of two back-to-back owls. With an elliptical mouth, a contracted neck and an oval belly, this jia has two bird-wings engraved in relief on both sides, which, together with a beak on each side, form the shape of two owls. Below the bottom of the belly, there are 4 four-edged tapered feet, with the ends casting outward. There is an arc-shaped cover, with a half-ring-shaped knob in the middle. This kind of knob is very popular in the bronze wares of the late Shang Dynasty. On each side of the knob, there is a square column, with sloping-roof-shaped top, and decorated with beast face patterns on its four sides.

Bronze Jia with Beast Face Patterns

Origin: Late Shang Dynasty
Height: 34 cm
Hammer Price: RMB 777,400
Name of Auction Company: Chongyuan International
Date of Transaction: 2006-10-05

Jia was used to pour wine into tripod, and was used to heat wine as well. According to the archaeological discoveries, bronze jia is always unearthed together with bronze tripod. It is recorded in the Book of Rites, that "those who are respected most use tripod, while those who are less respected use jia". This jia has a wide-flared mouth, a long neck, round shoulders and three pouched legs, with a pair of mushroom-topped columns on the rim. There is a beast-head-shaped handle on one side. The belly is decorated with beast face patterns, with the edges of the legs as its central lines. The neck is decorated with triangle patterns, and the shoulder with a circle of sloping thunder patterns.

Bronze Zhi with Owl-shaped Patterns

Origin: Late Shang Dynasty
Height: 32 cm
Hammer Price: RMB 3,960,000
Name of Auction Company: Chinese Cultural Relics
Date of Transaction: 2007-06-24

Zhi, a wine vessel first appeared in the late Shang Dynasty, and was popular in the early Western Zhou Dynasty, can be divided into two major categories: round zhi and elliptic zhi. This object has a wide-flared mouth, a deep belly and a ring foot. The cover of this zhi is divided into four sloping sides by four edges, and looks like the roof of the palace of the Shang Dynasty. The cover and the belly are decorated with owl-shaped patterns, with the head in the center and two wings folded aside. A similar object is preserved in the Asian Art Museum of San Francisco. Legend has it that this zhi was bought by a senior administrator of Minsheng corporation at the price of 500 silver dollars. Another similar object was transferred at the price of USD 8,100,000 in New York.

Bronze Zhi with Beast Face Patterns

Origin: Western Zhou Dynasty
Height: 16.6 cm
Hammer Price: RMB 506,680
Name of Auction Company: Hong Kong Christie's
Date of Transaction: 2003-07-07

Zhi is a wine vessel used in ancient times, shaped like tripod, but smaller in size. It was originated from the water container made of beast horn in ancient times. There are generally two types of zhi, namely, oblate zhi and round zhi. Zheng Xuan noted in the Book of Rites, that vessel with the capacity of 3 litres can be called zhi. This object, ellipsoid in shape, has a flared mouth, a contracted neck, a bulged-out belly and ring foot. The object is decorated with beast mast patterns on its belly, and has horn-shaped protrusions on the area below the neck. The same decoration can be found in the bronze ge (an ancient cooking tripod with hollow legs) unearthed from Liulihe of Beijing, as well as the bronze you (a wine vessel for holding wine, with a handle passing over the cover) unearthed from Hengyang of Hunan.

Bronze Tripod with Beast Face Patterns (two pieces)

Origin: Western Zhou Dynasty

Height: 18.9 cm

Hammer Price: RMB 991,800

Name of Auction Company: Chongyuan International

Date of Transaction: 2008-07-26

Tripod, the wine vessel in ancient times, was very popular in the Shang Dynasty, and became rare in and after the Western Zhou Dynasty. The earliest bronze tripod was found from the relics of the Erlitou Culture. According to the records in books of antique collection, tripod is widely used to show respect to the god, to communicate with the immortal, or to feast friends, in occasions like ceremony of boy's coming of age, marriage ceremony, funeral ceremony, etc. Archaeological discoveries have shown that tripod is the most commonly used ritual object. This tripod has a long spout and a pointed tail, with two mushroom-shaped columns near the spout. It also has a deep belly, a round bottom and three three-edged feet, with a beast-head-shaped handle on one side. The area below the rim is decorated with triangle patterns, while the belly is with beast face patterns, with thunder -and-cloud patterns as background. These two tripods, with the same design and decoration, must be cast in the same place.

Bronze Tripod with Beast Face Patterns (two pieces)

Origin: Qing Dynasty

Height: 17.5 cm

Hammer Price: RMB 79,200

Name of Auction Company: Beijing Hanhai

Date of Transaction: 2006-06-26

These two tripods were once used by Emperor Qianlong in sacrificial ceremonies. With an oval mouth and a deep belly, the tripod has two upright columns and three long feet, with decoration of beast face patterns on the belly. On the bottom of the tripod, there are inscriptions of "made in the Qianlong Era of the Qing Dynasty" engraved in seal characters. It is recorded in the Archive of the Qing Dynasty, that "on April 25th of the 13th year of Qianlong Era, Treasure Bai Shixiu forwarded the wood models of ritual objects to Emperor Qianlong. His Majesty ordered that the inscriptions should be made. On the May 2nd Bai forwarded images of ritual objects to the Emperor, and his Majesty ordered that the bronze wares should be made by Prince Zhuang, and the objects should be ready before various sacrificial ceremonies". Based on this record, we know that the bronze ritual objects should be made in exact number, with no reserves.

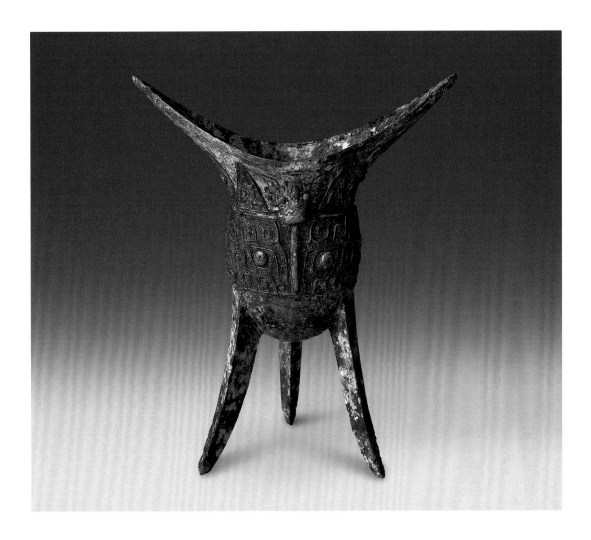

Bronze Jiao with Beast Face Patterns

Origin: Early Western Zhou Dynasty
Height: 22 cm
Hammer Price: RMB 1,552,500
Name of Auction Company: Chongyuan International
Date of Transaction: 2008-04-12

Jiao, with extended symmetric rim but without capped columns, is an ancient wine vessel similar in form to tripod. It got its name in the Song Dynasty. According to the Book of Rites, in the sacrificial ceremony, zhi is used by the most respected, while jiao is by the less respected. This jiao has an arc-shaped mouth, a deep belly, a round bottom and three three-edged feet, with a beast-head-shaped handle on one side. The area below the rim is decorated with triangle banana-leaf patterns, while the inner surface of the belly is decorated with cloud patterns and beast face patterns. This jiao, with ingenious design and delicate decoration, is similar to the Fuding Jiao unearthed from Gansu Province in 1967.

Bronze Gu with Beast Face Patterns

Origin: Late Shang Dynasty

Height: 29 cm

Hammer Price: RMB 313,200

Name of Auction Company: Chongyuan International

Date of Transaction: 2008-07-26

Gu is the goblet of ancient times. Gu and tripod were basic associated bronze wares in the Shang Dynasty, and were always unearthed together. Some of the gus were unearthed together with jias. Both in the tomb No.3 of Baijiazhuang in Zhengzhou City, and in the tomb No.338 of Xiaotun, 2 gus, 2 tripods and 2 jias were found together. Wine vessels were attached great attention to in the Shang Dynasty, and there were bronze wine vessels, as well as pottery wine vessels at that time. Gu, together with tripod and jia, was found in most of the tombs from this period of time. These vine vessels, as a set, represent different social status of the tomb owner, as the better in quality and the more in quantity, the higher the social status they have. This gu, big in size, has a wide-flared mouth, a slightly bulged-out belly and a high ring foot, with a round rim under the foot. The belly is decorated with beast face patterns, and the ring foot is with dragon patterns. All the patterns consist of thunder-and-cloud patterns.

Bronze Gu with Beast Face Patterns

Origin: Late Shang Dynasty
Height: 27.5 cm
Hammer Price: RMB 231,000
Name of Auction Company: China Guardian
Date of Transaction: 2006-06-03

Gu is an ancient wine vessel, various in design and popularly used in the Shang and Zhou Dynasties. Gu from the early and middle Shang Dynasty is thick and short, with a cross-shaped hole in the ring foot; while the gu from the late Shang Dynasty and early Western Zhou Dynasty is slim and long, with or without a cross-shaped hole in the ring foot. The gu from this period is thick in its matrix, and is decorated with patterns of beast face, cicada and banana leaf. Gu gradually disappeared after the late Western Zhou Dynasty. This gu has a wide-flared mouth, an upright belly, a high and outward ring foot, with a straight rim on the edge of the foot. There are four edges crossing its belly and foot. The article is decorated with patterns of cloud and thunder, banana leaf, cicada, silkworm, beast face and dragon. There are inscriptions of five Chinese characters on the foot. It is said that this gu belongs to the collections of Japanese collectors.

Bronze Gu with Beast-Face-like Patterns

Origin: Song Dynasty

Height: 31.8 cm

Hammer Price: RMB 56,000

Name of Auction Company: China Guardian

Date of Transaction: 2007-09-15

What archaeologists referred as "gu" was named first in the Song Dynasty. As the inscription on the gu doesn't mention its official name, it cannot be confirmed that this kind of article is "gu" recorded in ancient books. However, it is reliable to categorize gu to the wine vessel. In the Song Dynasty, it was popular for the governmental organizations to produce bronze wares imitating ancient style. This gu, with a wide-flared mouth, a vertical belly, and a high and outward ring foot attached with an upright rim around, has four edges crossing its belly and ring foot. The whole item is decorated with separated beast face patterns with the cloud-and-thunder patterns as the background. In the Song Dynasty, gu gradually became the article of appreciation for the literati, or the display for the royal families, besides the fact that it had become the object of collection and research.

Gilt Bronze Gu with Beast Face Patterns and the Inscription of "Made by Hu Wenming"

Origin: Reign of Emperor Wanli,Ming Dynasty
Height: 17.5 cm
Hammer Price: RMB 216,240
Name of Auction Company: Hong Kong Sotheby's
Date of Transaction: 2005-10-23

Gu is a wine vessel in ancient times. This gu, with a wide-flared mouth in the shape of trumpet and a contracted belly, has a high and out-flared ring foot in the shape of two-layered stage. The whole item is divided into three parts from the top to the bottom. The upper part is decorated with banana-leaf patterns, with transformed beast face patterns in the middle; the middle and lower parts have edges, inscribed different beast face patterns in relief. The joint areas of the beast face patterns, neck, belly, and ring foot, as well as the bottom of the foot are gilded. This gu is a typical imitation of the bronze gu in the Shang Dynasty. With the slim shape, splendid gilding and complicated design, this article is a masterpiece of the bronze wares in the Ming Dynasty. There are four Chinese seal characters inscribed on the bottom, which says "made by Hu Wenming". Hu Wenming was a famous designer and producer of bronzewares in the Wanli Era of the Ming Dynasty. He was born in Songjiang County. He was very experienced in making bronze stoves and bronze human figures. The bronze wares made by him were called "Hu Bronze wares" and were treasured by the people of that time.

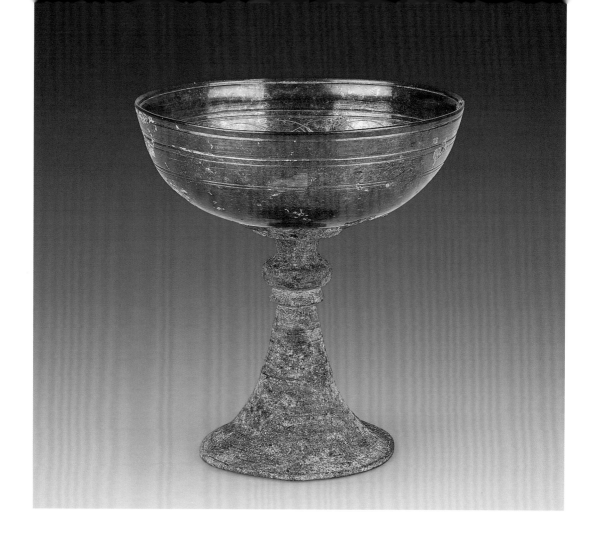

Bronze Cup with Lotus-petal Patterns

Origin: Tang Dynasty   Height: 10 cm
Hammer Price: RMB 27,500
Name of Auction Company: Liaoning Zone
Date of Transaction: 2006-10-26

Cup is the vessel for holding wine or water. This cup is made up of a semi-sphere bowl and a trumpet-shaped foot, with the decoration of two rounds of bow-string patterns. The inner surface of the bowl is decorated with lotus-petal patterns carved in intaglio. Lotus-petal patterns was very popular in ancient times. It first appeared in the Spring and Autumn Period, and was popularly used from the Southern and Northern Dynasties to the Song Dynasty. Lotus-petal patterns was used as the decoration of the covers in the Spring and Autumn Period and Warring States Period; while in the period from the Wei and Jin Dynasties to the Sui Dynasty, lotus-petal patterns was used to decorate the bellies of the bronze wares, or sometimes it was divided into several layers to decorate the neck, belly and foot, which provides the whole article a magnificent ornament. In the Tang and Song Dynasties, lotus-petal patterns was engraved by knife or through module. This cup is beautiful, dignified and well designed; however, some parts of the cup are corroded seriously by the rust.

Bronze Jian with Intertwining Dragon Patterns

Origin: Spring and Autumn Period

Height: 40 cm

Hammer Price: RMB 1,879,200

Name of Auction Company: Chongyuan International

Date of Transaction: 2008-07-26

Jian is the big-sized vessel for holding water. According to the documentary records and archaeological discoveries, jian had the following three usages in ancient times: before the bronze mirror came into being, jian could be used as mirrors, since the water hold will reflect images; jian could be used as bath tubs; jian could also be used to hold ice or iced food. This jian has a square rim, a huge mouth, a contracted erect neck and a short ring foot, with a belly bulged out. There are four ears located equally on four sides of the rim. The ears are shaped as tigers' heads holding rings in mouths. The neck and the belly of this article are decorated with intertwining dragon patterns. The patterns can be divided into three parts, with the upper part being narrow, middle part being wide, and lower part being wide triangles. The intertwining dragon patterns are complicated and exquisite, with the bodies of the dragons closely intertwined. This jian is similar to those two jians of king Fu Chai of Wu preserved in Shanghai Museum and the other one in Capital Museum. One unique feature of this jian is its tiger-head-shaped ears. The decorative patterns, as the wings being stressed and the bodies of the dragons being somewhat neglected, are also called wing patterns. This kind of patterns is produced by stamping module continuously. The stamping module can be found if observing carefully.

Bronze Bathing Fou with Cloud Patterns

Origin: Spring and Autumn Period
Height: 27 cm
Hammer Price: RMB 141,024
Name of Auction Company: Hong Kong Sino Art
Date of Transaction: 2006-11-25

Fou is an ancient vessel for holding water. Bathing fou is the ritual object used in taking bath. People in the early Qin Dynasty had the habit of washing hair once every three days, and taking bath once every five days. In the Han Dynasty, there was a one-day break every five days, called "Bath holiday". Due to hot and humid weather, ancient people in Yangtze River basin bathed more frequently. Noblemen in Chu Kingdom thus made a set of ritual objects for taking bath, and the bathing fou was one of them. This fou has an upright mouth, a folded rim, round shoulders, a bulged belly and a flat bottom, with a short ring foot attached to it. There are a pair of semi-ring beast-shaped ears on both sides of its shoulder, with the decoration of triangle cloud patterns and flame patterns.

Bronze Basin with Dragon and Phoenix Patternss

Origin: Spring and Autumn Period
Height: 30 cm
Hammer Price: RMB 253,340
Name of Auction Company: Hong Kong Christie's
Date of Transaction: 2003-07-07

Basin is the vessel for holding materials or for washing. It can also be used in the ritual ceremony. In the Book of Ritoo, it is recorded that "This is the sacrifice made to the Old Lady, with the materials contained in the basin, and the vase is the common wine-jar". It is also explained that this Old Lady is just the first one to make food, not the fire god himself. The sacrificial ceremony thus was not so respected, judging from the food contained in the basin and wine in the wine-jar. According to the archaeological discoveries, bronze basins were commonly found in the tombs of noblemen. As bronze basin is not a ritual object for noblemen, it can be concluded that these basins are for practical use. This basin has a wide-flared mouth, a wide rim, folded shoulders and a contracted belly, attached with a pair of semi-ring string-shaped ears on both sides. There are inscriptions of "Made by Zishuyingnei for the offsprings" on the surface of the basin.

Bronze Basin with Waterfowl Patterns

Origin: Yuan Dynasty
Diameter: 48.2 cm
Hammer Price: RMB 77,000
Name of Auction Company: China Guardian
Date of Transaction: 2001-04-25

This basin is huge in size, and has a folded rim. There is an image of waterfowls in lotus pond, with the patterns of lotus, lotus roots, canes, mandarin ducks, dragonflies and grass. The folded rim is also decorated with patterns of flowers. The whole article, with complicated design and exquisite inscription, is a masterpiece of the bronze ware in the Yuan Dynasty.

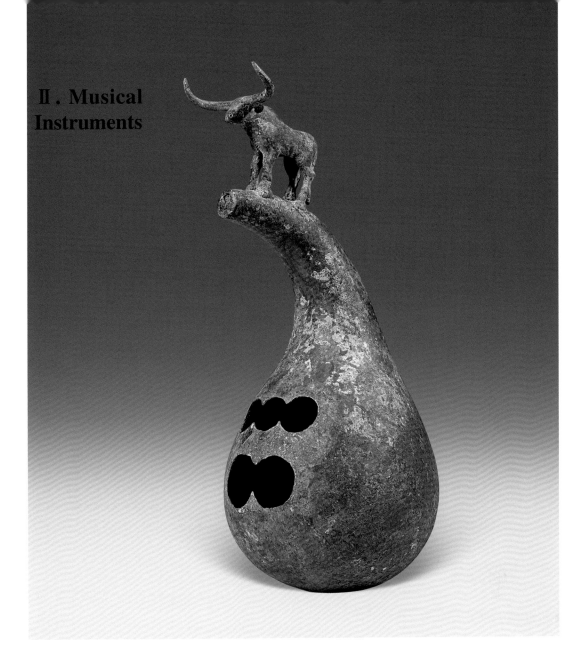

II. Musical Instruments

Bronze Gourd-shaped Sheng with the Sculpture of a Standing Ox

Origin: Warring States Period

Height: 28.7 cm

Hammer Price: RMB 106,800

Name of Auction Company: Chongyuan International

Date of Transaction: 2008-07-26

This article has an arc stem with the sculpture of a standing ox on the top, and with a hole for playing. The lower part of the article is sphere shaped, with two rows of holes on the surface. There are thress holes on the upper part, while two on the lower part. This sheng is similar to the gourd-shaped sheng unearthed in Lijiashan of Yunnan Province. And it should be the bronze musical instrument of the cthnic minorities of this area.

Bronze Musical Bells with Dragon Patterns (four pieces)

Origin: Spring and Autumn Period

Hight: 48 cm,43.5 cm,39.5 cm,38 cm

Hammer Price: RMB 4,554,000

Name of Auction Company: Chongyuan International

Date of Transaction: 2008-04-12

These four musical bells belong to one set of percussion instruments, with the same design and decorative patterns, but various size. The bells are in the shape of closed-tiles, with straight mouths. Each bell has a knob in the shape of two dragons standing on both sides. Two dragons, with the heads turned over and teeth outward, are connected with a rectangle bar. The bodies of the dragons are decorated with strip-like scale patterns. The belly is decorated with patterns of cloud and intertwining dragon. On the surface of each bell, there are 36 nipple-shaped protrusions in the shape of winding dragon. All the four bells, exquisite in engraving and complicated in design, are precious ancient bronze musical instruments.

Gold-and-silver-inlaid Bronze Bell with Geometrical Patterns

Origin: Qin Dynasty

Hight: 12.5 cm

Hammer Price: RMB 267,000

Name of Auction Company: Chongyuan International

Date of Transaction: 2008-07-26

The knob of the bell is in the shape of two dragons, with a U-shaped bar connecting the upward mouths of two dragons, and the whole knob is decorated with rhombic patterns and geometric patterns. The bell has a flat top. And with two corners of the mouth slightly bulged out, the whole article is in the shape of an ellipse. The end of the corners of the mouth is contracted inward. There are panels of nipple-shaped protrusions on the surface of the bell. And the area between the panels is decorated with diamond-shaped geometric patterns. The top area between lines of protrusions, and the other parts of the bell are decorated with spiral cloud patterns and transformed dragon patterns. All the patterns are inlaid with silver and gold. This bell is similar to the Yuefu Bell unearthed from the Mausoleum of the First Emperor of Qin in shape and decoration.

Bronze Zheng with Beast Face Patterns

Origin: Song Dynasty
Hight: 39 cm
Hammer Price: RMB 132,000
Name of Auction Company:
Tianjin Emperor's Ferry
Date of Transaction: 2005-06-16

Zheng is a small bell-shaped percussion instrument in ancient times. The Book of Songs has songs like"Zheng will lead the soldiers to be quite while drum will lead them to move". In the ancient battlefield, thousands of soldiers would, under the order of the commander, move forward or backward, attack or defend as a whole. Zheng would act as the tool to express the orders of the commander. Several zhengs, different in size, could be combined together to be played in ritual ceremony or feast. This zheng is decorated with cloud-and-thunder patterns on the top, with projecting beast face patterns in the central area, joint pearl patterns and string patterns on the knob, and has no decoration in the central belly area. Royal court was fond of imitational ritual objects from ancient times, which caused officials and noble families to follow this trend. This zheng is an imitation of the bronze zheng in the Western Zhou Dynasty. The rosewood holder was equipped by a collector of the Qing Dynasty.

Gilt Zhonglü Chime with Cloud and Dragon Patternss

Origin: Qing Dynasty
Hight: 21 cm
Hammer Price: RMB 29,526,750
Name of Auction Company: Hong Kong Christie's
Date of Transaction: 2008-05-27

Chime is one kind of ancient musical instrument. Emperor Kangxi of the Qing Dynasty respected teachers and attached great importance to Confucian ideas. He   ordered one set of chime to be built as the court ritual musical instruments based on the ritual ceremony of the Zhou Dynasty. The whole set of chime consists of 16 bells, which are same in size but various in thickness, representing 12 different notes. The notes, from the lowest one to the highest one, are: Huangzhong, Dalü, Taicu, Jiazhong, Guxi, Zhonglü, Ruibin, Lingzhong, Yize, Nanlü, Wuyi and Yingzhong. The chimes were played during ceremonies at the imperial altars for the great events, such as worship ceremony to Heaven and Earth, sacrificial ceremony in ancestral temple, formal banquets and state rites. In these ceremonies, the bells, setting on the tall wood bases, would play harmonious ritual music with Huangzhong being the basic tone. Witnessed by the emperor and other high-ranking officials, the chime, together with other ancient Chinese ritual musical instruments, such as bells, drums, would fully exhibit the grandness, sanctity and the absolute power of the emperor. The whole set of this chime, with its majestic design, splendid colour, and exquisite design, present the craftsmanship of the bronzewares in the Qing Dynasty.

III. Weapons

Bronze Dagger-axe with Beast Face Patterns

Origin: Western Zhou Dynasty
Length: 19.5 cm
Hammer Price: RMB 95,200
Name of Auction Company:
International Auction of China
Date of Transaction: 2009-11-13

Dagger-axe was a weapon to hook-cut or peck widely used from the Shang Dynasty to the Han Dynasty, especially during the period of the early Qin Dynasty. The standard dagger-axe consists of dagger, shaft and bronze buckle. The dagger axe can be classified as short dagger-axe and long dagger-axe for different usages in battlefield, based on the length of the shaft. This dagger-axe, with a short, wide and dull blade, and high relief decoration of beast face patterns on the surface, is probably used as a ritual object.

Bronze Sword with Diamond-shaped Patterns

Origin: Warring States Period
Length: 52 cm   Hammer Price: RMB 320,400
Name of Auction Company: Chongyuan International
Date of Transaction: 2008-07-26

In the chapter of weapons of Book of Explanation, it is recorded that "Sword is used to defend oneself in abnormal situation". It is also recorded in ancient books, that, in ancient times, emperors were supposed to wear hats and carry swords at the age of twenty; princes at the age of thirty; senior officials at the age of forty; however, slaves were not allowed to wear hats, and were permitted to carry a sword only when it was needed. This sword has long raised ridges on both sides, with blades arc-shaped and converged to one point at the end of the sword. The surface is decorated with diamond-shapod patterns, just like the sword of Yue's King Gou Jian unearthed from Jiangling, Hubei Province. Unlike other unearthed swords, this sword has a sheath in good condition.

Gilt Bronze Knife with Dragon Patterns

Origin: Qing Dynasty
Length: 107 cm
Hammer Price: RMB 418,000
Name of Auction Company: Beijing Hanhai
Date of Transaction: 2004-06-28

Bronze knife, as a weapon, was first discovered in the Shang Dynasty in China, with the blade always in arc shape. In the Qing Dynasty, waist knives and knives holding-with-two-hands were widely used in battlefield. Waist knives, with the upper part straight and lower part narrow and in arc shape, were commonly used by the cavalrymen. Knives holding-with-two-hands, on the other hand with a long blade and big size, were used by the infantry. Short knives were the most commonly used weapon in a in the Ming and Qing Dynasties. In the Qing Dynasty, emperors attached great importance to the military power. And the imperial court administration might produce weapons like guns, cannons, bows and knive, for emperors, or for emperors to award officials. This knife is equipped with sheath, which is gold-coated and decorated with dragon patterns. The knife and the sheath are exquisite, vigorous and luxurious.

IV. Bronze Mirrors

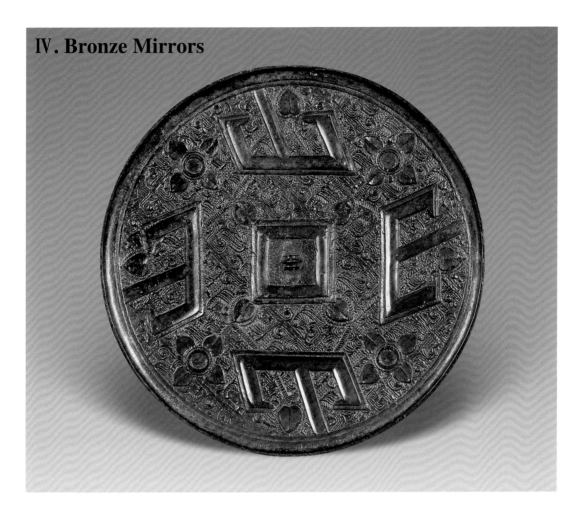

Bronze Mirror with Four W-shaped Patterns

Origin: Warring States Period

Diameter: 13.8 cm

Hammer Price: RMB 55,000

Name of Auction Company: China Guardian

Date of Transaction: 2006-06-04

    Bronze mirrors in the Warring States Period are always decorated with W-shaped patterns. There might be three, four, five or six W-shaped patterns on the back of the mirror, with the decoration of four W-shaped patterns being the most common one. A lot of bronze mirrors with four W-shaped patterns were unearthed from the tomb of Kingdom of Chu in Changsha, Hunan Province. This mirror, round in shape, has a three-stringed knob, with intaglio quadrangle around it. There is a leaf patterns on each corner of the quadrangle. The major decoration of this mirror is four W-shaped patterns, with the bottom of each patterns paralleled with each side of the quadrangle. These four W-shaped patterns are alternated by four flower patterns. These flower patterns are connected with the leaf patterns on the corners of the quadrangle by lines. W resembles mountains in Chinese characters in shape, which represents stability, tranquility and fertility, and is widely used to decorate bronze mirrors.

Bronze Mirror with Three Dragon Patterns

Origin: Warring States Period
Diameter: 18.2 cm
Hammer Price: RMB 16,500
Name of Auction Company: China Guardian
Date of Transaction: 2005-11-06

This mirror has a three-stringed knob, setting on a round knob base. Around the knob, there is an intaglio cloud-patterns-decorated circular arc and a narrow oblique-line-patterns-decorated circular arc. The major decoration of this mirror is three intertwining dragons, which have small heads and opening mouths, each with a long horn at the back side of the head. On the flanks of the dragons, there are interwining patterns forming the wings of the dragons. The whole design is complicated and smooth, fully embodying the advanced technology of bronze casting in the Warring States Period.

Bronze Mirror with Rhomb Patterns

Origin: Warring States Period
Diameter: 11.1 cm
Hammer Price: RMB 24,200
Name of Auction Company: China Guardian
Date of Transaction: 2005-05-15

    This mirror has a three-stringed knob, setting on a square base. The back of the mirror is decorated with four symmetrical rhomb patterns, which divide the feather-like ground patterns into several parts. Some mirrors of the same category have eight rhomb patterns, with a flower patterns inside. This kind of mirror was popular for a short period of time, and was therefore not largely produced. However, this mirror was a typical one from the Kingdom of Chu. Together with other bronze mirrors of the Kingdom of Chu, this mirror exhibits the cultural character and artistic favor of the Warring States Period.

Bronze Mirror with Linked Arc and Dragon Patterns

Origin: Warring States Period

Diameter: 16.6 cm

Hammer Price: RMB 70,000

Name of Auction Company: China Guardian

Date of Transaction: 2006-06-04

Linked arc patterns were popularly used in the Warring States Period and the Han Dynasty. Mirrors with linked arc patterns in the Warring States Period are always round in shape, with six, seven, eight, nine, ten, eleven, or twelve intaglio arcs linked to form a circus. The eight-arc mirror is the most common one. Mirrors with linked arc patterns in the Warring States Period could be divided into three categories, namely, mirrors with no decorative patterns, mirrors with cloud-and-thunder ground patterns, and mirrors with cloud-and-thunder and dragon patterns. This mirror has a three-stringed knob, which is encircled by an intaglio circus. Eight acentric arcs are connected one by one, with the cloud-and-thunder patterns as its ground patterns. There is a dragon, mouth open, eyes bulged out and body twisted, in the area between the arcs connected. Four small dragons, body bended and head turned back, are inside the arc. The whole article, with the fine designed patterns, fully embodies the advanced casting technology of the time.

Bronze Mirror with Nipple Patterns

Origin: Han Dynasty
Diameter: 11.2 cm
Hammer Price: RMB 13,750
Name of Auction Company: China Guardian
Date of Transaction: 2006-11-23

This mirror, round in shape, has a knob in the shape of continuous hills, surrounded by four nipples located on a circular string. There are six small nipples between the four nipples. The small nipples are connected by three-stringed patterns, and are adorned with 16 linked arcs outside. Nipple patterns is also called nebular patterns, as the formation of the nipples is regarded to represent the formation of the star and cloud. However, the prevailing understanding about this patterns is that it is formed by the twisted body of the animal or bird. Nipple patterns were very popular in the Western Han Dynasty. The antitype of the nipple patterns is discovered in the Han Dynasty tomb No.9 in Xujiawan of Shanxi Province, which reveals that this patterns is formed by the small humps on the twisted body of dragon. The mirror, excavated from Hongqingcun of Shanxi Province in 1953, is decorated with dragon patterns. The body of the dragon is full of nipples, which makes this mirror with the densest nipples ever discovered.

Bronze Mirror with Grass-and-leaf Patterns

Origin: Han Dynasty

Diameter: 10.5 cm

Hammer Price: RMB 3,520

Name of Auction Company: China Guardian

Date of Transaction: 2005-05-15

Grass and leaf, being of exuberant vitality, were widely used to decorate bronze mirrors in ancient China. Mirror with grass-and-leaf patterns was one of the most popular kind of mirrors in the Han Dynasty, and can be divided into three sub-categories, namely, mirrors with four-nipple and grass-and-leaf patterns; mirrors with four-nipple, grass-and-leaf and peddle patterns; and mirrors with grass-and-leaf and standard patterns. The back of the mirror is decorated with four or eight leaves, and some might be decorated with four-nipple patterns, dragon patterns or standard patterns. The knob base of this kind of mirror is always decorated with four-leaves patterns, and some might with string patterns or prostrate dragon patterns. This kind of mirror always has a square around the knob and the knob base, some might have inscriptions around the square. The edge of the mirror is always decorated with linked arcs, mostly, sixteen linked arcs. This mirror, has a round knob and inscriptions of eight Chinese Characters, which means "the sun brings light to the whole world".

Zhao Ming Bronze Mirror

Origin: Han Dynasty
Diameter: 19.5 cm
Hammer Price: RMB 69,000
Name of Auction Company: Chongyuan International
Date of Transaction: 2006-05-02

This mirror has a round knob, setting on a base which consists of twelve linked beads. With a wide and clear edge, this mirror has two circles of inscriptions concentrically, which are separated by a circle of short-stripe patterns. The inner circle of inscriptions has 24 Chinese Characters, which means "One should be integrated inward and properly dressed outward. One should be ambitious and loyal, but not arrogant and aggressive". The outer circle of inscriptions is featured for its style of calligraphy, which is half seal style, and half official script. This inscription reflects the fact that the style of Chinese Characters was transforming from seal style to official script at that time.

Bronze Mirror with Boju (Game Board) Patterns

Origin: Han Dynasty
Diameter: 18.8 cm
Hammer Price: RMB 55,000
Name of Auction Company: Shanghai Zhengde
Date of Transaction: 2006-06-30

Bronze mirror with boju patterns, also named as TLV bronze mirror, is actually the reflection of the popular game played at that time. According to the Book of the Han Dynasty, "People gathered, setting the board of game, singing and dancing, to offer sacrifices to the goodness", which suggests that both the common people and the god were crazy about the game at that time. A similar bronze mirror preserved in the Henan Provincial Museum was engraved with the Chinese Characters "Carved with a game board patterns to dispel misfortune", which revealed that the main purpose of the boju patterns on the mirror was ritual. This mirror has a semi-circular knob and a round knob base, surrounded by 12 nipples, which stand for the 12 earthly branches. The main decorative patterns is a game board, which sets black tortoises, red phoenixes, green dragons, white tigers and winged men on line.

Bronze Mirror with Decoration of Painted Chariot and Horses

Origin: Han Dynasty
Diameter: 20.8 cm
Hammer Price: RMB 30,000
Name of Auction Company: Shanghai Zhengde
Date of Transaction: 2006-06-30

This mirror has a semi-sphere knob and a knob base with linked bead patterns. There are four nipples outside the knob and the base, which divide the mirror into four sections. Section one is the image of the Goddess of Western Heaven, served by five winged men; section two is the God of the Eastern Heaven, served by three winged men; section three is a green dragon turning its head back; and the last section is a chariot and three horses. This chariot with horses should be the one specially for the disposal of the Goddess of Western Heaven. What is interesting are the inscriptions on the head of one of the horses, which read "Gong Ma"(meaning male horses).

Bronze Mirror with Dragon and Tiger Patternss

Origin: Han Dynasty

Diameter: 11.8 cm

Hammer Price: RMB 57,200

Name of Auction Company: Shanghai Zhengde

Date of Transaction: 2006-06-30

This mirror, has a semi-sphere knob and a round knob base. The major decorative patterns of the mirror are two dragons and one tiger. Both the dragons and the tiger, mouths and eyes widely open, are fine engraved and vividly exhibit the vigour and strength of the animal. There are inscriptions of 25 Chinese Characters on this mirror. The whole inscription is lined in a circle around the knob base. Outside the circle of inscription, there are two circles of comb patterns, with one circle of wave patterns in the middle. The whole article, being well preserved, is the masterpiece of the same category of bronze mirrors.

Bronze Mirror with Design of Mythical Beasts Standing in Rows

Origin: Han Dynasty
Diameter: 14.5 cm
Hammer Price: RMB 82,500
Name of Auction Company: Shanghai Zhengde
Date of Transaction: 2006-06-30

This mirror has a big and flat knob and a round knob base, with the images of gods and mysterious animals set around. On the left side, there is the image of the God of Eastern Heaven; on the right side, the image of the Goddess of Western Heaven;on the upper side, images of three gods, as one of them, serving the other two, is listening to their lectures; on the lower side, there are three other gods, as the one in the middle is playing musical instrument, and the other two are listening to the music. What is hard to understand is that four out of the eight gods engraved on this mirrors are wearing hats with three W-shaped patterns. Bronze mirror with the design of mysterious beasts in rows first appeared in the middle and late of the Eastern Han Dynasty, and had become one of the most important category of bronze mirror ever since then. With rows of gods and mysterious beasts, the whole mirror resembles the shrine in grotto.

Bronze Mirror with Design of Mythical Beasts, Produced in the 4th year of Pakang Era

Origin: Jin Dynasty

Diameter: 13.8 cm   Hammer Price: RMB 25,000

Name of Auction Company: China Guardian

Date of Transaction: 2006-06-04

This mirror has a round and flat knob, setting on a round knob base. The major decorative patterns of this mirror are mysterious beasts, which are encircled by the patterns of semi-spheres and squares alternatively. The edge of the mirror is engraved with inscriptions. What is unique is that the inscription has exact date with it, 6th February of the 4th year of Dakang Era. Dakang is the reign title of Emperor Wudi in the Jin Dynasty, and the fourth year of Dakang Era is the year of 283 AD.

Bronze Mirror with Round Flower Patterns

Origin: Sui Dynasty

Diameter: 20 cm   Hammer Price: RMB 154,000

Name of Auction Company: China Guardian

Date of Transaction: 2005-05-15

The mirror has a big and round knob, surrounded by 6 rounded flower patterns. Outside the flower patterns, there are a circle of inscriptions, which say that these flowers will bring prosperity, fortune and peace to the world. Rounded flower is also called Baoxiang Flower. Baoxiang is used by the Buddhist to address Buddha respectfully. Therefore, Baoxiang Flower, representing sanity, solemnity and beauty, was widely used in various patterns since the popularization of the Buddhism in the Wei, Jin, and Southern and Northern Dynasties. This patterns has combined the features of lotus, rose and chrysanthemum, and has created the feeling of auspiciousness and happiness.

Bronze Mirror with Inscriptions of"Chuan Wen Ren Shou"

Origin: Sui Dynasty

Diameter: 24.2 cm   Hammer Price: RMB 3,850,000

Name of Auction Company: Shanghai Zhengde

Date of Transaction: 2006-06-30

This mirror has a semi-sphere-shaped knob and a knob base with lotus patterns. Four lotus-shaped beads divide the major surface into four parts, and each part is engraved in high relief with different images. The first part is a Persian with a horse and the second part is a person from the Western Regions training a lion. The third part is a Persian with a beast, which has four claws and stands like a dragon. The fourth part is the phoenix and the Chinese unicorn. Outside the major decoration, there is a circle of inscriptions, which explain that this mirror was produced in the Reign of Renshou. Renshou is the reign title of Emperor Wendi in the Sui Dynasty. Outside the circle of the inscription, there is a circle of 12 auspicious beasts, intervened by flower and grass patterns. The auspicious beasts are: auspicious fish, white tiger, flying phoenix, auspicious beast, etc. At the edge of the mirror, there is a circle of saw-cutting patterns and a circle of honeysuckle patterns. The whole mirror vividly exhibits the culture exchange between the Western and the Eastern in the Sui and Tang Dynasties.

Bronze Mirror with Auspicious Beast and Grape Patternss

Origin: Tang Dynasty

Diameter: 17.7 cm   Hammer Price: RMB 880,000

Name of Auction Company: Shanghai Zhengde

Date of Transaction: 2006-06-30

Grape was the fruit first introduced to China during the Han Dynasty when Zhang Qian was sent to the Western Regions as an envoy. This fruit, growing in cluster, was liked by the Chinese people as it symbolizes fertility and vigor. Bronze craftsmen in the Tang Dynasty widely used grapes and vein scrolls, together with beasts, birds, bees and butterflies, to decorate bronze mirrors. This mirror, without a knob base, is divided into two sections: the inner section and the outer section. The inner section is decorated with five clusters of vein scrolls and six auspicious beasts. The vein scrolls are used to decorate the marginal area, leaving the main area for the auspicious beasts. The auspicious beasts are vividly engraved, and fully exhibit the advanced casting craftsmanship of the time. The decoration of the outer section is similar to that of the inner section, with the grapes and vein scrolls being background patterns, giving prominence to the beasts. There are altogether eight beasts on the outer section, namely, two wild boars, two phoenixes, two deer and two cranes. Except for phoenix, other beasts are rarely used as auspicious beasts to decorate this kind of bronze mirror. The edge of the mirror is decorated with a circle of round flower patterns. Bronze mirror with auspicious beast patterns and grape patterns is the most precious and finest in the bronze mirrors of the Tang Dynasty.

Bronze Mirror with Celestial-being-flying Patterns

Origin: Tang Dynasty
Diameter: 12.3 cm
Hammer Price: RMB 11,000
Name of Auction Company: China Guardian
Date of Transaction: 2005-11-06

This mirror has a round knob, with the whole article in the shape of a eight-pedal sunflower. The inner section of the mirror is decorated with four celestial beings flying with cranes or Chinese unicorns. The outer section is decorated with bee patterns and lotus leaf patterns alternatively.

Bronze Mirror with Dragon Patterns

Origin: Tang Dynasty
Diameter: 15.7 cm
Hammer Price: RMB 17,050
Name of Auction Company: China Guardian
Date of Transaction: 2006-11-23

Dragon patterns is widely used to decorate bronze mirrors. In the Warring States Period, curled up dragon patterns and intertwined dragon patterns were used in the bronze mirrors. In the Han Dynasty, green dragon of the Four Auspicious Beasts was used in the bronze mirrors. In the Tang Dynasty, curled-up dragon was widely used. The singular dragon is engraved vividly on this mirror. With the eyes and mouths widely open, the dragon fully exhibits its vigour and grandiosity. The dragon is always accompanied by auspicious clouds. In ancient China, dragon symbolized the emperor. And the curled-up dragon with auspicious clouds symbolized "true dragon and son of Heaven". This mirror, in the shape of sunflower, has a round knob with a dragon around it. Accompanied by four auspicious clouds, the dragon is turning its head back, with a pearl in mouth. The mirror has been well preserved.

Bronze Mirror Decorated by Mother-of-Pearl

Origin: Tang Dynasty
Diameter: 23 cm
Hammer Price: RMB 250,000
Name of Auction Company: Beijing Xinding
Date of Transaction: 2006-04-16

Mother-of-pearl, or Luodian, refers to the shell of sea shellfish. This shell was widely used as material to decorate bronze mirrors in the thriving period of the Tang Dynasty. The shell is first cut and grinded into thin and various shapes, and then is inlaid on the back of the mirror according to the design. The shell, being naturally shining and colorful, provides a stunning visual effect for the mirror, and also fully exhibits the features of the prime of the Tang Dynasty. This mirror, in silver white color, has a semi-sphere knob, surrounded by flowers, leaves and auspicious beasts. The flowers, leaves and auspicious beasts are made of the mother-of-pearl, which provides an elegant and exquisite feeling for the mirror.

Bronze Mirror with Moon Palace Patterns

Origin: Tang Dynasty

Diameter: 14.3 cm

Hammer Price: RMD 63,800

Name of Auction Company: Shanghai Zhengde

Date of Transaction: 2006-06-30

This mirror has a knob in the shape of a prostrate beast, half surrounded by a cassia tree. On the left side of the tree, there stands Lady Chang E Goddess of the Moon ; while on the right side, the Jade Rabbit is pounding medicine in a mortar. Both the Lady Chang E and the Jade Rabbit are vividly engraved, which fully exhibit the advanced casting technology of the time. It is unusual to have a knob in the shape of a prostrate beast, since other bronze mirrors would take the trunk of the cassia tree as the knob. The legend of the Moon Palace has been recorded ever since the Warring States Period.

Bronze Mirror with Dragonfly Patterns

Origin: Song Dynasty

Diameter: 15 cm

Hammer Price: RMB 5,280

Name of Auction Company: China Guardian

Date of Transaction: 2005-05-15

This mirror has a semi-sphere knob, setting on a flower-shaped knob base. The major decorative patterns are four dragonflies flying off the knob in four different directions, alternating with four elegant flowers. Bronze mirrors from the Song Dynasty can be described as fresh, simple and elegant, full of the beauty of daily life. Applying the design of landscape painting, the mirrors are always unsymmetrical. Various flowers and folklores appeared on the bronze mirrors of that time.

Bronze Mirror Produced by Family Shi of Huzhou

Origin: Song Dynasty
Diameter: 13 cm
Hammer Price: RMB 35,200
Name of Auction Company: China Guardian
Date of Transaction: 2005-11-06

The mirror is in shape of a square, with four angles being dented. There is a small and round knob in the middle of the mirror, with a crane and a slim bamboo on each side. The image of a pond is located below the knob. What makes it unique are the inscriptions on the central area above the knob, which mean this mirror is made by a craftman in Huzhou, with the family name of Shi. In the Song Dynasty, Huzhou area was very famous in producing fine bronze mirrors. A lot of craftmen, with different family names, gathered here. Among them, those with the family names like Shi, Li, Lu, Wan, Huang, Jiang, Fu, Han, Ding and Wang were the famous ones. Craftmen with the family name of Shi were of the greatest reputation. These craftmen would like to use the inscriptions to identify the mirrors made by themselves and to avoid others to forgo. These kinds of inscriptions, just like a brand name, tell a lot of information about the mirror itself, such as the location of the shop, the family name and the ranking among the siblings of the producer, or the honorable family history of manufacturing bronze mirrors.

Bronze Mirror with Makara Patterns

Origin: Liao Dynasty
Diameter: 19.2 cm
Hammer Price: RMB 101,200
Name of Auction Company: China Guardian
Date of Transaction: 2006-06-04

This Mirror, in the shape of a eight-petal sunflower, has a round knob. The major decorative patterns of the mirror is a makara patterns, with the head of the beast turning back with a pearl in mouth. There are cloud patterns on the flanks of the beast, and flame patterns over the head of it. Makara is a sea-creature in Indian mythology. It is generally depicted as the beast having a long trunk, sharp teeth and a fish tail. Makara is regarded as the god of the river and the ultimate source of the life. Makara was introduced into China along with the cultural exchange between the Western and the Eastern. Makara patterns is also called fish-dragon patterns in China.

Bronze Mirror with Double-fish Patterns

Origin: Jin Dynasty
Diameter: 16.1 cm
Hammer Price: RMB 28,600
Name of Auction Company: China Guardian
Date of Transaction: 2006-06-04

This mirror, round-shaped, has a round knob, with two fishes in relief with the head and the tail linked. The fish, including the head, eyes, gills, scales and fins, is vividly and clearly engraved, around with waterweed patterns. Double-fish symbolizes fertility and plenty, thus was greatly loved by the Nüzhen peole. In the Jin Dynasty, dancers danced with the hold of mirrors with fish patterns in court, which was called mirror dancing. It was once recorded that carps were transferred from dragons, and those with a Chinese character "wang"(king) on the foreheads were real gods. In ancient China, those who passed imperial examinations and got posts in the government were refered as the carps which had leaped through the dragon's gate.

Bronze Mirror with Dragon Patterns Made in the 4th Year of Zhiyuan Era

Origin: Yuan Dynasty

Diameter: 22.5 cm

Hammer Price: RMB 68,200

Name of Auction Company: China Guardian

Date of Transaction: 2006-06-04

The mirror has a semi-sphere knob, with a square around. Inside the square, there are inscriptions of four Chinese characters, which mean this mirror was made in the 4th year of Zhiyuan Era. There are flaming ball patterns on the flanks of the square. And two dragon patterns are engraved in relief on and below the square. The dragons are decorated with cloud patterns, lotus leaf patterns and flower branch patterns. There are two Zhiyuan Eras in the Yuan Dynasty. One was of Emperor Kublai which lasted from 1264 to 1294; the other was of Emperor Shundi, which lasted from 1335 to 1340. Judging from the information of the same batch of antiques unearthed, this mirror should be produced in the 4th year of Zhiyuan Era of Emperor Shundi.

Bronze Mirror Made in the 22nd Year of Hongwu Era

Origin: Ming Dynasty
Diameter: 13.2 cm
Hammer Price: RMB 8,800
Name of Auction Company: China Guardian
Date of Transaction: 2006-06-04

    This mirror, round-shaped, has a mountain-shaped knob. There is a dragon engraved in relief on the back of the mirror, with the dragon's head below the knob, its body winding upward and its claws stretching out. There are cloud patterns and wave patterns around the dragon. On the left side of the knob, there are inscriptions of Chinese Characters, which identify that this mirror was made in the 22nd year of Hongwu Era (AD 1389).

V. Religious statues and appliances

Bronze Statue of Sitting Xuanwu God

Origin: Ming Dynasty   Height: 73 cm
Hammer Price: RMB 748,800
Name of Auction Company: Hong Kong Sotheby's
Date of Transaction: 2006-10-08

Xuanwu God, posthumously known as True Warrior Grand Emperor, is one of the high-ranking Taoist deities. Legend has it that Xuanwu was originally a prince of Jingle State. He was born with overwhelming power, and was awarded a sword by a god during a trip to the East China Sea. He went to remote Wudang Mountain of Hubei Province for practice, and became a god himself after 42 years of cultivation. As "Xuan" was avoided as a taboo in the Song Dynasty, he had been addressed as Zhenwu from then on. He was always depicted as a warrior with hair dishevelled, wearing dark clothes, holding a sword and stepping on the snake and turtle. Xuanwu was greatly respected among the people after the Ming Dynasty. This statue, with Xuanwu sitting on the throne and holding a jade tablet, has vividly exhibited the majestic and amiable expressions of the Xuanwu God.

Gilt Bronze Statue of Sitting Sun Simiao (King of Medicine)

Origin: Ming Dynasty   Height: 32.4 cm
Hammer Price: RMB 418,000
Name of Auction Company: Beijing Hanhai
Date of Transaction: 2006-12-12

Sun Simiao was a famous traditional Chinese medicine doctor in the Sui and Tang Dynasties. He became a famous doctor when he was still young. Emperor Wendi of the Sui Dynasty once summoned him for an interview, and provided him a post as the official lecturer of the Imperial College, but was refused by him. Sun Simiao refused to be an official in the Tang Dynasty, and never stopped his research on Chinese medicine till his old age. Keeping learning from the other doctors, the folks and the doctors from foreign countries, he spent more than 10 years writing two books—Beijinyaofang of 30 volumes (essential formulas for emergencies worth one thousand pieces of gold) and Qianjinfang (supplement to the formulas with the worth of one thousand pieces of gold) of 30 volumes, which were collectively called Qianjinfang (formulas worth one thousand pieces of gold). These books are the milestones in the history of Chinese medicine, systematically summarizing medical achievements before and in the Tang Dynasty. This book is regarded as the earliest encyclopedia of clinical medicine in China, and has greatly influenced the medical development afterwards. Sun Simiao was called King of Chinese medicine after his death.

Bronze Statue of Zhang Xian

Origin: Ming Dynasty
Height: 49 cm
Hammer Price: RMB 187,000
Name of Auction Company: China Guardian
Date of Transaction: 2003-11-26

This is the statue of Zhang Xian, who is engraved with a round face and dignified deportment. The hat, clothes and the decorative ribbons of the statue are lifelike. Bearing a bag for pellets, the statue's right hand is holding a pellet, and the left hand is supposed to hold a catapult which has been lost. Zhang Xian had been a deity popular in Sichuan Province since the Ming Dynasty. According to the Haicheng County Annals, "Couples who are sterile would enshrine and worship Zhang Xian. In the portrait, Zhang Xian protects his children who are around himself from Celestial Dog (a legendary evil from ancient China) with his bows and arrows. The shrine of Zhang Xian is always set on the back door of the bedroom, with the arrow aiming outwards. Ladies who have male offsprings would make their offerings to Zhang Xian on the first and fifteenth day of every lunar month". Another legend has it that Zhang Xian was actually Meng Chang, the King of Sichuan. After Meng Chang was killed by Emperor Taizu of the Song Dynasty, his wife Madam Huarui became an imperial concubine of Taizu. To commemorate her husband Madam Huarui kept the the portrait of Meng Chang in her room, and lied to Taizu that this was the portrait of Zhang Xian, the deity to turn to for male offsprings in Sichuan area.

Bronze Statue of Liu Hai

Origin: Qing Dynasty
Height: 21 cm
Hammer Price: RMB 132,000
Name of Auction Company:
Shanghai Jiatai
Date of Transaction:
2005-06-05

Legend has it that there was a golden toad hiding in the well in Changde City. There was shining light coming from the well to the heaven at night sometimes. It is said that those who were blessed could go to heaven and became immortal along with this shining light. An honest and filial young person named Liu Hai lived near that well. Liu Hai lived a simple life with his mother, and earned their living by cutting firewood in the hills. A fairy fox fell in love with Liu Hai, and transformed to be a beautiful girl to marry him. After the marriage, this fairy fox spitted out a white pellet and asked Liu Hai to use it as the bait to hook the golden toad. Once the golden toad swallowed the white pellet, Liu Hai climbed the back of the toad, went to heaven and became immortal. This statue is designed based on this legend. Liu Hai, with hair on the shoulders and clothes gently flowing, is designed vividly to stand on the back of the toad, with one hand holding coins and a treasure box, and the other holding a leaf of lotus to cover his head. There are inscriptions of "produced in the Reign of Qianlong of the Qing Dynasty" on the statue.

Bronze Buddha Statue
Made For the Meng Family

Origin: Northern Wei Dynasty
Height: 15 cm
Hammer Price: RMB 227,240
Name of Auction Company:
Chongyuan International
Date of Transaction:
2006-05-02

This bronze statue is similar to the bronze Bhikkuni Buddha statue made by Fa Du in the 22nd year of Taihe Era in the Northern Wei Dynasty. Two statues have the same robes, the same halos on the head and back, and the same design of three Buddhas in the halo of the back. The only difference is that this statue has two more Buddha sculptures in the back halo, which is similar to another sitting stone Buddha statue preserved in USA Nelson-Atkins Museum of Art that was made in the 18th year of Taihe Era in the Northern Wei Dynasty. There are inscriptions on the stand identifying that this statue was made for King of Meng and his family. This article, with unsophisticated design and simple material, is original and rare among bronze statues this category.

Gilt Bronze Statue of Sakyamuni Buddha and Two of His Disciples

Origin:
Northern Zhou Dynasty
Height: 17.5 cm
Hammer Price: RMB 275,000
Name of Auction Company:
Tianjin Cultural Relics
Date of Transaction:
2003-08-27

This statue consists of one main Buddha and two serving gods. The main Buddha has fleshy cheeks, long eyebrows and a high hair bun, and wears a loose garment that covers shoulders and is decorated with long bands. The garment is multilayered, and is tied a knob in front. The elbow of the right hand is folded in front of the chest and the left arm is holding up. The main Buddha is believed to be Sakyamuni, with two of his disciples standing on the lotus stages with bare feet. According to the records on Buddhist scriptures, Sakyamuni, the founder of the Buddhism was born as the prince of Kingdom of Kapilavastu. At the age of 29(or 19, according to other versions of the records), witnessing ageing, sickness, death and all of the sufferings in the life of human being, Sakyamuni left his palace and his life as a prince, and went to seek the ultimate solutions to these problems. At the age of 35, Sakyamuni attained enlightenment under a Bodhi tree, and founded Buddhism. At the age of 80, Sakyamuni entered nirvana or the final deathless state, in the city of Kusinayara.

Bronze Statue of Guanyin Bodhisattva(Avalokitesvara)

Origin: Liao Dynasty
Height: 30 cm
Hammer Price: RMB 60,500
Name of Auction Company:
Zhonghongxin International
Date of Transaction: 2001-06-29

This is a bronze statue of standing Guanyin Bodhisattva, who wears a high cap. The cap is delicately decorated with metamorphosed Buddha and rolling grass patterns. Guanyin has a broad forehead and fleshy cheeks, and holds a bunch of flowers. With eyes looking down, Guanyin has a benignant smile on her composed face. Guanyin is standing on the lotus stage with her bare feet. Slightly influenced by the realistic tendency of the Song Dynasty, the bronze statues of the Liao Dynasty mainly imitated the style of the statues of the Tang Dynasty, especially the grotto statues of the Tang Dynasty. This kind of imitation can be detected from the miniature design of the giant statues, which keeps the sculpture being lofty. The ethnic flavour of the Liao Dynasty can also be observed in this statue, such as the fleshy cheeks which are fond of by the Khitan people, and the high cap which is the reflection of the clothing of the Khitan nobles. To match the comparatively larger upper body of the statue, the lotus stage is designed multilayered, with the end of the large leaves raising outward. The Liao Dynasty was founded by the Khitan people in the Northern China. Buddhism had become popular in the Liao Dynasty since Emperor Taizong, and prevailed in the reigns of Emperor Shengzong, Xingzong and Daozong. It is recorded that Taizong once set Guanyin as the protection Buddha of his family. Ever since then, Guanyin had become the common and best image of the bronze statues in the Liao Dynasty.

Gilt Bronze Statue of Sitting Guanyin Bodhisattva(Avalokitesvara)

Origin: Ming Dynasty   Height: 33 cm
Hammer Price: RMB 460,000
Name of Auction Company: Chongyuan International
Date of Transaction: 2006-10-05

Guanyin, with fleshy cheeks and long beards, is sitting with legs crossed and soles upward, and holding a ruyi(an S-shaped ornamental object symbolizing good luck) with both hands. Guanyin is wearing a treasure cap, a double-collared garment, and a necklace of jade and pearls. According to the doctrine of Buddhism, Buddha is described as transcending genders. However, because of the influence of the secular world, Buddha has some gender features in the Buddhist scriptures and Buddha related artistic articles. In the early Indian Buddhism, Buddha was depicted as male, which is why the Buddha was referred as "Man of Merits" ,"Great man",or "Vigorous and powerful husband" in the Buddhist scriptures. The statues of Buddha in the early Indian Buddhism were wearing beards. This bronze statue, obviously, is produced based on the early doctrine of the Buddhist scripture.

Gilt Bronze Statue of Amitabha Buddha

Origin: Ming Dynasty   Height: 51 cm
Hammer Price: RMB 1,452,000
Name of Auction Company: Liaoning International
Date of Transaction: 2001-12-10

Amitabha is originally a term in Sanskrit, which, in its Chinese translation, means infinite light and infinite life. Amitabha Buddha is one of the most respected Buddhas among Chinese Buddhism disciples. It is believed that once you chant "Amitabha", you will be protected by Amitabha and will be led to the Western Heaven by him after death, which is why almost every family makes offerings to him and chants "Amitabha". This statue, with a fleshy and round face and downward-drawing upper eyelids, has vividly exhibited the benevolence and solemnity of the Amitabha Buddha. Amitabha Buddha is wearing a toga of monks with a swastika mark in the front of its chest, and a cassock that covers shoulders outside. Two hands are holding a Dhyana mudra gesture. The whole article is well preserved and the gilding technology is fully exhibited.

Gilt Bronze Statue of Green Tara

Origin: Ming Dynasty　　*Height: 19.5 cm*
Hammer Price: RMB 825,000
Name of Auction Company: Tianjin Cultural Relics
Date of Transaction: 2003-08-28

According to the Origin of Tara, Guanyin Bodhisattva had saved numerous people before the measureless eons. However, she could not bear to see the suffering of the people leaving behind the other day. She cried, and tears became lotuses, which turned to be 21 Taras afterwards. Buddha in this statue is wearing a treasure cap, with pearls engraved in relief at the edges. The cap extends to the ears, where it is in the shape of fans. The necklace consists of a series of rings, which are decorated with three pearls. The Buddha is holding the stems of lotuses, with the left hand gestured in mudra of teaching, and the right hand gestured in mudra of supreme generosity. One leg of the Buddha is folded, while the other is stepping on the lotus stage. There are inscriptions engraved on the lotus stage, which say "produced in the Yongle Era of the Ming Dynasty".

Gilt Bronze Statue of Supreme Pleasure Vajra(Chakrasamvara)

Origin: Ming Dynasty   Height: 35 cm
Hammer Price: RMB 1,760,000
Name of Auction Company: Beijing Council
Date of Transaction: 2006-11-23

Supreme Pleasure Vajra, or Supreme Please Buddha King, is the fundamental honoured Buddha of all the four schools of Tibetan Buddhism. It is said that Supreme Pleasure Vajra includes 72 forms, and the most common forms are the four-faced and twelve-armed form, one-faced and two-armed form and one-faced and six-armed form. This statue applies the four-faced and twelve-armed form. Four faces represent reducing disaster, increasing blessing, loving and obedience, and each face has different expressions. There are three eyes on each face, which stand for the abilities to look into the past, present and the future. The Vajra wears a tiger skin skirt, and a necklace made of fifty skull heads, which represent fifty sanskrit letters. One foot of the Vajra is stepping on the Great Freedom God, and the other on the Great Freedom Goddess, indicating that achievement is accomplished by suppressing one's anger, greed and etc. The lotus stage is engraved with inscriptions in Sanskrit letters. The major two hands gestured in mudra, with one hand holding a ring and the other holding a pestle. The other hands are holding various weapons. The holo behind the head is decorated with skull heads and Vajra pestles. This article, vividly and clearly engraved, and finely cast, is one of the masterpieces of the bronze statues of the Buddha in the early Ming Dynasty.

Gilt Bronze Statue of Padmasambhava

Origin: Ming Dynasty Height: 20 cm
Hammer Price: RMB 242,000
Name of Auction Company: Tianjin Cultural Relics
Date of Transaction: 2006-10-05

  Padmasambhava was born in Kingdom of Udayan in ancient India. In the year 761, he was invited to transmit Vajrayana Buddhism to Tibet area. Therefore, he is regarded as the founder of Tibetan Vajrayana Buddhism. He was respected as Guru Rinpoche or a second Buddha Padmasambhava. With a typical treasure cap with folded rim on his head, he wears a cross-collared robe inside and a kasaya outside. One hand of the Buddha is holding a bowl with the decoration of skull head patterns, and the other holding a Vajra staff. The Padmasamhava is sitting with legs crossed and soles upward. The expression of Padmasamhava is composed and dignified. The lotus stage consists of two-layered lotus leaves, with the cloud patterns on the heads of lotus leaves. This article is one of the masterpieces of the same categories of bronze wares.

Gilt Bronze Statue of Manjushri from Xuande Era

Origin: Ming Dynasty   Height: 26 cm
THammer Price: RMB 1,958,000
Name of Auction Company: Beijing Council
Date of Transaction: 2006-11-23

　　This is a bronze statue of Manjushri. Wearing a treasure cap on head, Manjushri is engraved with a broad forehead and fleshy cheeks, with the head inclined slightly to one side. The ribbons near the ears are decorated with delicate linked rings. The Buddha is naked in the upper part of his body, wearing only a necklace with three ornaments of treasure as the pendants. The necklace, the waist belt and the wave-shaped smocking enhance each other's brightness and beauty. With two hands holding a mudra of teaching, manjushri is sitting on a two-layered lotus stage. The lotus stage is decorated with two circles of beads on each layer. Inscriptions which mean "produced in the Xuande Era of the Ming Dynasty", are engraved on the stage. Some erosion on the face, on the limbs of the Buddha and on the lotus stage indicates the material being rose copper.

Gilt Rose Copper Statue of Medicine Buddha

Origin: Ming Dynasty   Height: 37.5 cm
Hammer Price: RMB 660,000
Name of Auction Company: China Guardian
Date of Transaction: 2005-05-15

Medicine Buddha, also named Medicine Buddha Bhaishajyaguru, is described as a doctor who can cure deadly diseases. He is the hierarch of the eastern realm of pure Lapis Lazuli, where he is attended to by two groups of Buddhas symbolizing the sun and moon respectively. Medicine Buddha is respected by Chinese people as "Buddha that can disperse calamity and prolong life". This Medicine Buddha is engraved with a square face, wearing a high hair bun and topped with a pile of jewels. The eyes of the Buddha are looking down calmly at the ground. The Kasaya that Buddha wears covers only the left shoulder, with the right shoulder covered with extra cloth. Buddha is sitting on a lotus stage with legs crossed. His left hand holds an alm bowl in meditation mudra, and the right hand is in varada mudra. The inscription on the back of the lotus stage explains that this statue was made in the Xuande Era of the Ming Dynasty, and tells the cause of its making.

Gilt Bronze Statue of Birupa, the Mahasiddha

Origin: Ming Dynasty   Height: 28.5 cm

Hammer Price: RMB 330,000

Name of Auction Company: International Auction of China

Date of Transaction: 2005-08-13

Birupa is the most famous Mahasiddha in Tibetan Buddhism. The image of him has appeared in Han and Tibetan areas since the Yuan Dynasty. This statue reveals the most common image of him: with the hair being plaited and piled into a high hair bun, he is naked on the upper part of the body, which is decorated only with crossed necklaces of linked pearls. He wears a short skirt, with a silk belt around the waist and the right knee. He is sitting on a animal-skin-covered stool, with his left leg lying on the stool, and right leg putting up. His right hand is pointing up at something, while the left hand is pushing down the ground. This posture is connected with a legend about Birupa, which says that he has the ability to make the sun stop moving and cause the time stop at the moment.

Gilt Bronze Statue of Guanyin with Eleven Faces and One Thousand Hands

Origin: Qing Dynasty   Height: 53 cm
Hammer Price: RMB 743,500
Name of Auction Company: Chongyuan International
Date of Transaction: 2006-10-05

This Guanyin has 11 faces and 42 hands, with the main two hands holding together in front, and the rest 40 hands on both sides. As all the living creatures have 25 states in life, these 40 hands imply that Guanyin is able to protect all the living creatures in every state, hence the name of Guanyin with one thousand hands. Eleven faces represent eleven different expressions of Guanyin. The whole statue is full of the style of Tibetan Buddhism, which can be traced from Guanyin's high cap, the ear rings, the rings on the arms, the pearl and the necklace that Guanyin wears. The lotus stage and the halo, on the other hand are full of the flavor of Indian Buddhism. The outer edge of the halo is decorated with flower-and-leaf patterns, and a circle of connected vajra-pestal patterns is engraeve on the inner edge. When the Qing Dynasty was boomed in the 17th century, Tibetan Buddhism became popular in Eastern Mongolia area. In 1634, Nurhachi finally conquered Mongolia area. After that, Tibetan Buddhism became the religion believed by the emperors and the court. In the mid-Qing Dynasty, Tibetan Buddhism became influential in Tibet, Nepal and Kashmir areas. And the image of the Buddhism statues combined various genres and became colorful.

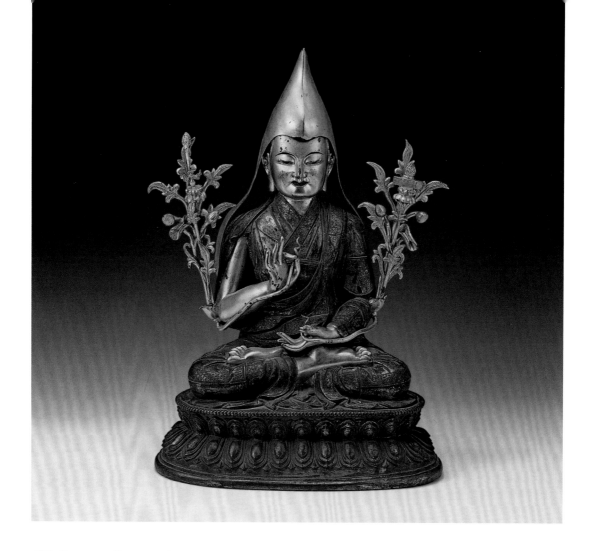

Gilt Bronze Statue of Tsongkhapa

Origin: Qing Dynasty   Height: 39 cm
Hammer Price: RMB 104,500
Name of Auction Company: Tianjin Cultural Relics
Date of Transaction: 2001-06-27

Wearing a peach-shaped monk hat, Tsongkhapa is symmetrially engraved. He is sitting on the lotus stage with legs crossed, with a gently smile on the face and hands holding a Buddha mudra. There are branches of lotus on each side of the shoulders. Tsongkhapa is the founder of Geluk School of Tibetan Buddhism. Tsongkhapa was born in Qinghai, and was initiated into Buddhism when he was three. At the age of 7, he left home and became a monk. After nine years of study of Buddhism, he went to Tibet at the age of 16 to disseminate Buddhism and became famous since then. Tsongkhapa intended to reform the Buddhism and asked his followers to wear yellow hat and abide by the doctrines of Tibetan Buddhism. Thus Geluk School is also called Yellow Hats School. In the 7th year of Yongle Era in the Ming Dynasty, he established Ganden Monastery and strove to stop the conflicts among different Buddhism schools. In the 12th year of the Hongwu Era in the Ming Dynasty, he was summoned for an interview in Beijing by Zhu Di, Emperor Chengzu. Tsongkhapa sent his disciples on his behalf to meet Emperor Chengzu. Tsongkhapa died in the 17th year of Yongle Era in Ganden Monastery.

Gilt Bronze Statue of the Beast that Protects Buddhism(one pair)

Origin: Ming Dynasty   Height: 30 cm   Length: 39 cm
Hammer Price: RMB 209,000
Name of Auction Company: Beijing Jiaxin
Date of Transaction: 2006-07-29

In legend, this beast is the creature that protects and upholds Buddhism. In the monastery of Tibetan Buddhism, there is always a golden ring in the middle of the roof, which has a beast on each side. This beast that protects Buddhism is also found outside the cave of the Mogao Grotto of Gansu Province, as well as the Qianfoyan of Qixia Mountain. In most of the cases, these beasts are in pairs, one male and one female. These two beasts that protect Buddhism, although the heads of which have been ruined, can be identified as two male ones, which embodies the influence of the Northern and Southern Dynasties. These two statues of the beast that protect Buddhism, large in size and gilded, should be located outside the monasteries or some religious sites.

Gilt Bronze Vajvakilaka

Origin: Ming Dynasty
Height: 24.3 cm
Hammer Price: RMB 1,980,000
Name of Auction Company: Beijing Hanhai
Date of Transaction: 2008-12-18

Vajvakilaka is originated from the nail that is used to fix tents. Vajvakilaka is called "purbhu" in Tibetan language, which is similar to vajra as a ritual article, and symbolizes the power to overcome all the evil creatures or hindrances. This bronze vajvakilaka can be divided into three parts. The upper part is a three-faced irate rajas. Three-faced irate rajas is normally regarded as the apotheosized image of the purbhu. Three faces share one high hair bun, which is red and in the shape of flame. There are three widely open eyes on each face, which represent the power to obtain three initial approaches to become a Buddhist believer. The flame-shaped moustache, the thick eyebrows and the sharp teeth, all exhibit the power of irate rajas to destroy the evil creatures and to resist temptations. The middle part and the handle consist of two symmetric patterns. These patterns resemble the braided fabric, and symbolize demons being chained. An inscription is engraved on this part, which means this vajvakilaka was made in the Yongle Era of the Ming Dynasty. The lower part consists of Makara and a trigone pestle. The snakes from the mouth of Makara symbolize the connection between Makara and snakes-and-dragons. In most of the ritual articles, Makara may be simplified into just a huge mouth, with the upper lip extended as long as the elephant's trunk. The trigone pestle stands for the power to enable people to get rid of the fetters of the outside and to obtain the mental freedom inside. This vajvakilaka, with shining color and complicated design, is the precious ritual article from the imperial court of the Ming Dynasty. This is one of the only two vajvakilakas that bear the inscriptions of being produced in the Yongle Era of the Ming Dynasty.

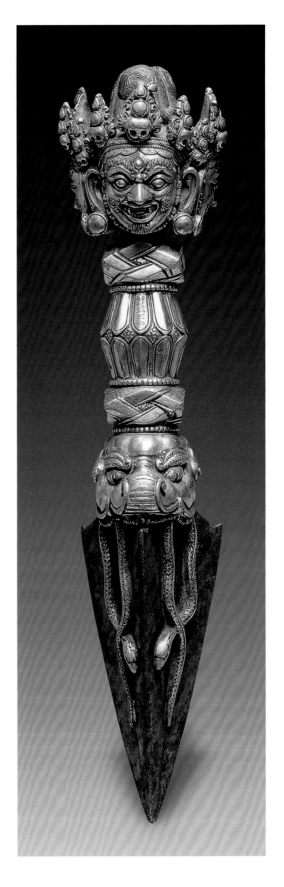

Gilt Bronze Statue of Lotus-shaped Mandala

Origin: Ming Dynasty   Height: 46 cm
Hammer Price: RMB 3,080,000
Name of Auction Company: Chengming International
Date of Transaction: 2005-09-17

Mandala is a Sanskrit term and originated from the Esoteric sect of Indian Buddhism, meaning the rite where Buddhas and their adherents gather. In the practice of ancient Esoteric Buddhism, square or round altars were built, with Buddhas enshrined herein and surrounded by adherents, to resist invasions of evil spirits, and that was the so-called mandala. The Buddha enshrined in this statue is Chakrasamvara, who, with several heads and arms, is holding religious tools and stepping on demons, representing the conquest of annoyances of human beings. Designed as an eight-petaled lotus, the statue is elaborately conceived and exquisitely carved.

VII. Others

Gilt Bronze Jar with Sea and Beast Patternss

Origin: Ming Dynasty
Diameter: 8.5 cm
Hammer Price: RMB 40,320
Name of Auction Company: Beijing Poly
Date of Transaction: 2008-10-12

This kind of jars was mainly used as containers of water for ink-stones. Usually placed on tables in studies, they are also ornamental objects, whose material, craft, shape, patterns and conception. must be compatible with the owners'tastes. This jar, with a contracted mouth, an outward-bulged belly, a flat bottom and sea and beast patterns on the surface, is finely decorated and gold-coated in delicate craftsmanship. It is a rare study appliance, symbolizing literators' pursuit of elegant life.

Ox-head-shaped Brush Pot

Origin: Ming Dynasty
Height: 9.5 cm
Hammer Price: RMB 605,000
Name of Auction Company: Beijing Hanhai
Date of Transaction: 2004-01-12

Brush pot is the most widely used holder for brushes, usually cylindric and made of various materials such as bamboo, wood, porcelain, lacquer, jade, ivory, etc. They were very popular among literators in ancient times for their artistic characters and cultural tastes. This brush pot is in the shape of an ox head in the front, which is, with wide open eyes and upright ears, very lively. It is inscribed with "made in Xuande Era of the Ming Dynasty". Qiu Yanzhi, who was globally celebrated for his collections of ancient Chinese porcelain, ever owned it in his later years.

Hill-shaped Pen Rack

Origin: Ming Dynasty

Height: 17.5 cm

Hammer Price: RMB 187,000

Name of Auction Company: China Guardian   Date of Transaction: 2000-11-06

Pen rack, with a history of over 1500 years, had already been commonly used in studies in the Tang Dynasty. Their materials varied from bronze to stone in the Song Dynasty, and were even more diversified in the Ming Dynasty, including coral, agate, crystal, porcelain, jade, etc. This pen rack is decorated with eighteen egrets and lotuses, supported by a rectangular pedestal with six ruyi-shaped feet. It is characterized by the delicate decoration and exquisite craftsmanship among its kinds.

Bronze Beast-shaped Paper weight

Origin: Ming Dynasty   Height: 9.5 cm

Hammer Price: RMB 156,800

Name of Auction Company:Xiling Yinshe

Date of Transaction: 2008-06-29

According to historical records, paper-weight has been used for over 1500 years up to now. This paperweight, purplish red and in the shape of an elephant, is inlaid with silver threads all over the body to imitate creases in the skin. The crouched elephants, with crooked legs, swinging tails, drooping ears, looking downwards and splashing trunk in the water, are in lively appearance, fluent lines and exquisite craft. It is inscribed with the name of Shi Sou, who lived in the late Ming Dynasty and was celebrated for his unequalled craftsmanship of making silver-inlaid bronze wares.

Box-shaped Four-footed Lamp

Origin: Western Han Dynasty
Height: 14 cm
Hammer Price: RMB 63,820
Name of Auction Company: Chongyuan International
Date of Transaction: 2006-10-05

As a lighting instrument, the lamp was used in daily lives as well as in ancestral temples. This lamp is in the shape of a box, whose cover is attached by a rod-like hinge, and half of the cover, with a beast-head holding ring design, can be opened up as a lamp tray. The box is oval, with a deep belly for containing lamp oil, beast-head holding ring designs on both sides, and four hoof-like feet at the bottom. The cover decorated with concave bow-string patterns is well preserved.

Cylindric Shell-storing Vessel with Five Oxen

Origin: Western Han Dynasty   Height: 24.5 cm

Hammer Price: RMB 1,097,600

Name of Auction Company: Beijing Zhongjia

Date of Transaction: 2010-05-09

Bronze shell-storing vessels, unique artifacts of the ancient Dian Kingdom, are of rather high aesthetic value. Their covers are decorated, in separated casting and welding craft, with many delicately carved solid statues which vary from people to animals. This vessel is cylindric and tri-footed, decorated with boating, zoomorphic and geometric patterns on the body and five oxen on the cover.

Bronze Iron with Eight-treasure Patterns

Origin: Qing Dynasty   Height: 17 cm
Hammer Price: RMB 88,000
Name of Auction Company:Tianjin Cultrual Relics
Date of Transaction: 2007-06-20

Bronze irons once were prevailed in the Han and Wei Dynasties, and had been continuously used until the 60s and 70s of the last century. They generally have round bellies and a wide mouth rim. This iron is characterized by the auspicious Tibetan Buddhist patterns carved all over its body, which are frequently used in Buddhism to symbolize good luck and imply the peaceful country and contented people.

Bronze Tiger Head

Origin: Reign of Emperor Qianlong,Qing Dynasty

Height: 31.9 cm

Hammer Price: RMB 16,371,435

Name of Auction Company: Hong Kong Sotheby's

Date of Transaction: 2000-05-02

Emperor Qianlong ever saw and was fascinated by baroque stonework, fountains and decorations in the pictures of western palaces, so decided to build a European-style palace in the Yuanmingyuan Garden. French priest Benoist, the mathematician and astronomer who had knowledge of hydraulics, was assigned to construct a similar fountain for the emperor. He then built a time-indicating fountain with which Emperor Qianlong was extremely satisfied. The twelve animal signs, having the heads of beasts and the bodies of human beings, were sitting beside two ponds in alternate permutation, representing the twelve moments within one day. Every day they in turn sprayed water to the ponds rotationally and endlessly, shifting every two hours, and sprayed simultaneously at high noon. Tiger, ox and monkey were all among the twelve time-indicating animal signs. The bronze tiger head is realistically lifelike in manner, line and decoration, and entirely unlike the traditional Chinese bronze wares which are massive, it is a good combination of Chinese and western elements. When the Anglo-French Allied Forces occupied Beijing in 1860, the fountain was ruined and heads of the animal signs were drifted to Europe.

Bronze Ox Head

Origin: Reign of Emperor Qianlong, Qing Dynasty
Height: 43.1 cm
Hammer Price: RMB 8,209,700
Name of Auction Company: Hong Kong Christie's
Date of Transaction: 2000-04-30

Ox is among the Chinese twelve animal signs. This bronze statue was originally placed in the Yuanmingyuan Garden as one of the twelve water-spraying apparatuses.

Bronze Monkey Head

Origin: Reign of Emperor Qianlong, Qing Dynasty

Height: 45.7 cm

Hammer Price: RMB 8,676,100

Name of Auction Company: Hong Kong Christie's

Date of Transaction: 2000-04-30

Monkey is among the Chinese twelve animal signs. This bronze ware was originally placed in the Yuanmingyuan Garden as one of the twelve water-spraying apparatuses.

Incense Burner with Dragon Patterns

Origin: Western Han Dynasty

Height: 22.5 cm

Hammer Price: RMB 187,920

Name of Auction Company:Chongyuan International

Date of Transaction: 2008-07-26

According to the cultural relics unearthed from the tomb of the Western Han Dynasty in Changsha, incense appliances were then often used to burn vanilla for banishing filth and purifying surroundings. This burner has a plane surface, a tall pedestal and ears in beast-head holding ring design on both sides of the belly. The cover is arched, with a ring handle on the top surrounded by open-carved dragon design and radial hollowed stripes. The belly and pedestal are decorated with convex bow-string patterns.

Bronze Civilian-Riding Censer

Origin: Ming Dynasty
Height: 40 cm
Hammer Price: RMB 90,720
Name of Auction Company: Zhejiang Poly
Date of Transaction: 2008-06-26

The horse, in concise and vivid shape, is richly and elaborately decorated, especially the saddle. The man riding on it wears a tall hat and a broad girdle, daring and energetic. The opening in the saddle connects with the hollow belly of the horse, and the civilian's arm is carved with cloud.

Gilt Beast-shaped Incense Burner (two pieces)

Origin: Qing Dynasty
Height: 17.5 cm
Hammer Price: RMB 220,000
Name of Auction Company: China Guardian
Date of Transaction: 2002-11-03

Gold-coated all over the body, this burner is in the shape of an auspicious beast whose head is elaborately designed as the cover, with four feet stepping on a coiled snake.

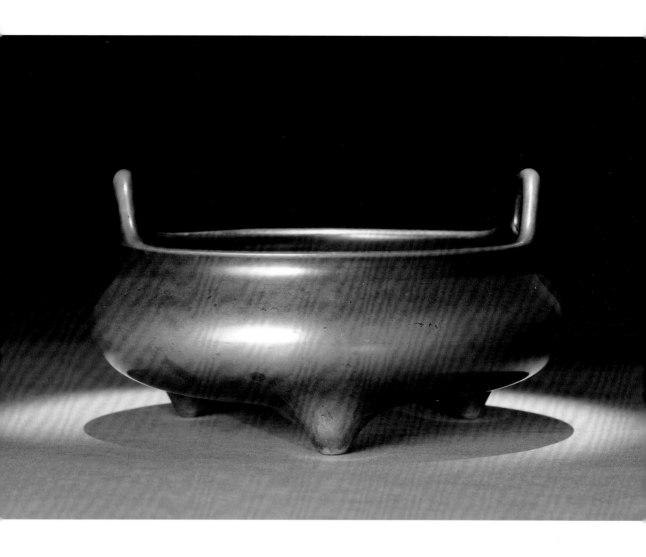

Tri-footed Bronze Stove

Origin: Reign of Emperor Shunzhi, Qing Dynasty

Mouth Diameter: 9.6 cm

Hammer Price: RMB 11,760,000

Name of Auction Company: Beijing Council

Date of Transaction: 2010-12-04

This stove, in regular shape, is an ideal combination of rusticity and exquisiteness. It has a slightly contracted mouth, upright ears on the mouth rim, a flat body, a bulged belly and three feet. The inscription cast on the bottom indicates that the stove was made in 1661, in the very year of which Emperor Shunzhi died of illness and Emperor Kangxi succeeded.

Bronze Rectangular Stove

Origin: Reign of Emperor Kangxi, Qing Dynasty
Mouth Diameter: 14 cm
Hammer Price: RMB 14,560,000
Name of Auction Company: Beijing Council
Date of Transaction: 2010-12-04

This stove has a rectangular body, vertical ears on both sides and four right-angled feet. It is extremely massive and according to the inscription cast on its bottom, can be regarded as a typical stove made by the Shi-family. With a square shape and clear edges and corners, it reveals masculinity and solemnity subtly.

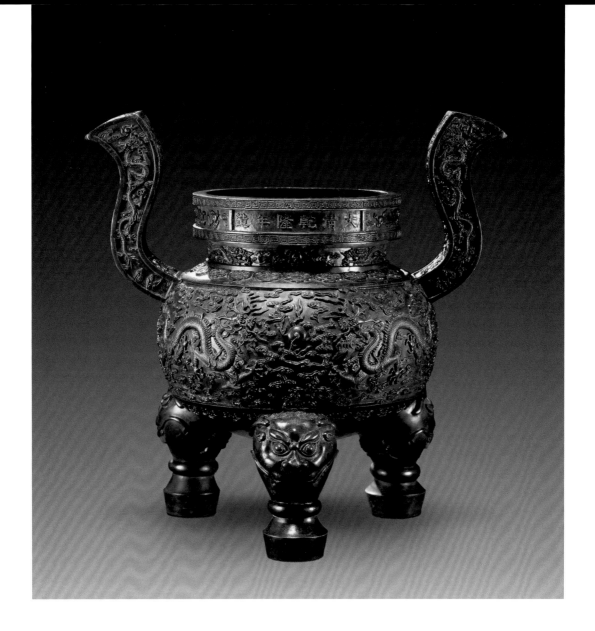

Bronze Censer with Cloud and Dragon Patternss

Origin: Qing Dynasty   Height: 37 cm
Hammer Price: RMB 2,352,000
Name of Auction Company: Beijing Poly
Date of Transaction: 2008-05-30

This censer has a contracted neck, a round belly, three beast-shaped legs and two long and high-rising ears on the upper belly. Characters cut in relief saying "made in Qianlong Era of the Qing Dynasty" are cast on the outside of the mouth rim. Its whole body is decorated with complicated and elaborate patterns: two dragons playing with a pearl patterns on the belly, cloud and dragon patterns on the neck and ears, and beast face patterns on the feet. The exquisite craftsmanship reveals the supremacy and luxury of royal sacrificial utensils.

Bronze Horse

Origin: Han Dynasty   Height: 43.8 cm
Hammer Price: RMB 896,000
Name of Auction Company: Liaoning International
Date of Transaction: 2008-06-22

    Chinese horse breeding had made great progress in the Han Dynasty, and there were a large number of horse images in sculptures and handicrafts at that time. According to the current unearthed relics, the horse figures in the Han Dynasty can be classified as the concrete one and the abstract one. The former follows the realistic style of the Qin Dynasty's Terra-Cotta Warriors, and the latter, attaching more importance to the expression of spiritual intention, uses exaggeration and deformation on the basis of concrete images and better reflects the aesthetic sentiment and artistic style of the Han Dynasty. This bronze horse, in well proportioned shape and dynamic rhythm, is the perfect integration of high intelligence and rich imagination, as well as romantic mind and excellent technique.

Bronze Persian-presenting-treasures Statue

Origin: Song Dynasty   Height: 15 cm
Hammer Price: RMB 89,600
Name of Auction Company: Beijing Hanhai
Date of Transaction: 2007-12-17

The statue, standing on two feet, with the left hand swinging downwards and the right hand holding high a piece of coral, is in a graceful gesture and of the typical Indian and Gandhara style. It wears coiled hair, a robe with a round neck and narrow sleeves, a waistband with a hanging water-bag and a dagger, and a short skirt with fine patterns. The statue was originally gold-coated, but now the gilt has mostly flaked off. From the Tang Dynasty to the Qing Dynasty, the ceremony of foreigners presenting treasures to Chinese governments had lasted for over a thousand years, which symbolized the prosperity and harmony of ancient China.

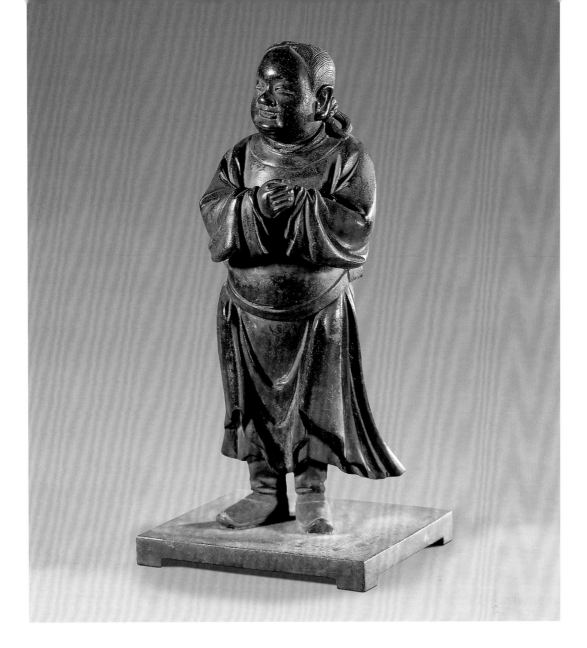

Bronze Standing Boy Statue

Origin: Yuan Dynasty
Height: 24.5 cm
Hammer Price: RMB 220,000
Name of Auction Company: China Guardian
Date of Transaction: 2003-11-26

The boy wears a round-necked robe, a waistband and boots, with hair parted from the middle and chignons hanging over the shoulder. The face is plump and broad, and the manner is naive and rustic. It was once coated with gold lacquer on the robe and red lacquer on the pedestal, all of which has nearly been peeled off now.

Bronze Chinese Unicorn

Origin: Qing Dynasty
Height: 34 cm
Hammer Price: RMB 190,400
Name of Auction Company: Shanghai Jiatai
Date of Transaction: 2006-06-23

Chinese unicorn, recorded in Chinese ancient books as the mount of gods, is generally treated as a kind of beneficient and auspicious beast. As an imaginary animal, it integrates in shape characteristics of various animals of which people are fond: a dragon-like head, deer-like horn, lion-like eyes, a tiger-like back, a bear-like waist, snake-like scales, an ox-like tail, horse-like hoofs, etc. This pair of statues, with raising heads, round eyes, open mouths, bare teeth, erect mane, stretched front-claws and squatted back-claws, exhibit their manners and power to a perfect extent. They are so delicately carved that even hair and scales are of meticulous workmanship.

Bronze Lion

Origin: Qing Dynasty
Height: 28.3 cm
Hammer Price: RMB 288,000
Name of Auction Company: Hong Kong Christie's
Date of Transaction: 2007-05-29

It was not until Zhang Qian's opening up of the Western Regions that the Chinese got to know the existence of the lion. Regarded as the king of all beasts and symbolizing might and stateliness, the lion was widely adopted in sculptures and patterns to guard gates, tombs or Buddha in ancient China. The lion playing with a silk-thread ball is a traditional propitious patterns. It is said by folk tales that the silk-thread ball is a huge pearl, with which the lion plays to calm itself down and give birth to the young lion wrapped in the ball, which represents producing offsprings in succession. The statues are in the shape of lions stepping on silk-thread balls, imposing and vivid, and must be placed beside gates as talismans.

Bronze Buffalo-herding Statue

Origin: Qing Dynasty

Height: 44 cm

Hammer Price: RMB 46,200

Name of Auction Company: Liaoning Zone

Date of Transaction: 2007-11-16

Cattle is an important subject of artistic creation. Cattle-herding has all along been lusted for by generations of literators for its far-reaching artistic conception, and the industriousness of cattle is also estrolled. In this statue, a buffalo paces ahead with a herder sitting on the back sideways, and is followed by a peasant shouldering farm tools. The work is lifelike and technically exquisite, depicting thoroughly the rural life in the southern regions of the Yangtze River.